Stop Chasing Start Living

Your Mind, Body, and Spirit Self-Care Transformation Guide

Take Care of, Invest in, and Empower Yourself First

Ellecia Clarke-Edwards

ISBN: 978-1-958404-58-4 (paperback)

BOOK PUBLISHING

Principles for Taking Care of, Investing in, and
Empowering Self

We were taught that self-care is Selfish; this book
will challenge that!

ACKNOWLEDGMENTS

I would like to thank God, who gave me the direct instruction to write this book. I give Him all the glory and the praise for affording me the strength to finish it.

I am so blessed and grateful to have friends, family members, and prayer partners who not only prayed and covered me while writing but also encouraged me during the process.

Special thanks to my awesome husband, who was very supportive during the writing process. You are a real gem!

TABLE OF CONTENTS

Acknowledgments..v

Introduction 11

Part A

Chapter 1: The Journey to Self-Transformation ..17

Stop Chasing 18

Start Living 20

Grounded in Self-Management............................. 21

The Self-Transformation Journey to Self-Care 23

The Self-Transformation Plan............................... 24

Self-Transformation Plan...................................... 28

How to Achieve Self-Transformation.................... 29

What is Self-Care? 31

Starting Your Self-Care Journey........................... 33

Chapter 2: Taking Care of Self............................41

Love Yourself First.. 42

Heal From the Root: Stop Cutting the Branches ... 43

Serving to be Seen 48

Three Tenets of Basic Self-Care (Think Well, Eat Well, Rest Well) 49

Tenet #1 - Think Well 50

Tenet #2 - Eat Well...52

Tenet #3 - Rest Well..69

Tune Into Yourself 78

Say "No" Gracefully (and Firmly): Cut Hypocrisy 80

Comfortably Disappoint Others 82

Meditation vs. Medication.....................................84

Chapter 3: Investing in Self First 87

Create a Personal Development Action Plan 90

Going Back to School...95

Invest Your Time Well..97

The ROI of Self-Improvement 99

Start Your Own Business 100

Read! Read! Read! 106

Chapter 4: Empowering Self...............................109

Remain Self-Empowered 110

Take Ownership of Your Inner-Power.................111

Lack Empowerment? Do Something About It!....112

Self-Empowerment and Self-Confidence.............114

Chapter 5: Empowered to Quit Toxicity 117

Knowing What You Want 118

Empowered to Quit Toxic Relationships............. 120

Marriage Toxicity 121

Don't Mold Your Partner in Your Image 126

Empowered to Quit Toxic WorkPlaces 128

Self-Care and the Corporate Community 130

The Self-Care and Work-Life Balancing Game .. 132

Part B

Chapter 6: Self-Care and the Word **139**

Physical Self-Care.. 140

Mental Self-Care.. 142

Talk to Someone 143

Emotional Self-Care... 144

Spiritual Self-Care 145

Financial Self-Care 149

Self-Care Plan 157

Self-Care Plan **158**

Implement Systems That Work **159**

Conclusion **163**

Reminder Tips on Self-care **165**

Appendix **169**

INTRODUCTION

S*top Chasing Start Living* is a book that will challenge you to focus on yourself for a change. What are you chasing that is currently draining your energy, stealing your time, and robbing you of manifesting your purpose? What are you chasing that is blocking your full mind, body, and spirit transformation?

In today's world, we are constantly bombarded with distractions. These distractions will pull you in many different directions, away from enjoying the present moment, away from your purpose, away from your self-care routines, etc. Whenever you are distracted, whenever you are chasing, you will lose sight of the significance of investing in your greatest resource – "YOU." Until you are able to properly TAKE CARE OF, INVEST IN AND EMPOWER YOURSELF, you will not be able to take care of or significantly impact someone's life.

This book will challenge some of the misconceptions and misunderstandings that we had growing up. We believed that someone "taking care of themselves first" translated to the person being selfish. The questions that will challenge that are "Can one pour out of an empty vessel? Can an unhealthy, disempowered, unmotivated person assist someone in need?" The simple fact is, you must fill up, charge up, pump up, gas up, and empower up yourself before you can be properly positioned to assist someone in need.

Think about it, if you work yourself sick or work yourself to death, what good are you to someone else? Undoubtedly, in this twenty-first century, the mass is becoming more conscious of the significance of self-care. More people now realize that they can actually say no to a request, take a week-long vacation and not feel guilty, and go to a restaurant and order something other than chicken. This revelation is now hitting a number of people like a ton of bricks, and now its acceptance will require a mindset shift. Oops, how difficult or easy will that be, since the matter of proper self-care is skewed from a sub-conscious level?

I was urged to write this book as I went through my own self-transformation and revelation that chasing too many things leaves you nowhere. Self-care was normally at the bottom of my list and would only get attended to "If I had the time to facilitate." In fact, believe it or not, my idea of self-care was having ice-cream on a Sunday.

Self-transformation involves some kind of action and requires both discipline and persistence. It requires structure and control so that "the transformation" can be maintained over the long haul.

Self-care is being in love with self. We do not take care of ourselves because we are not in love with ourselves. There is a reason why we as human beings push to go the extra mile in helping others. The reason behind this is that deep down, we have a need to be needed; Ouch! Sorry to be so blunt, but it is the truth. Do not get me wrong, we should certainly be of service to others, and it is a good thing, but when you harm yourself to be of service, that is where you have gone wrong. The Word of God does say you should "Love your neighbour as yourself" (see Mark 12:31).

I am so happy that you made the conscious decision to read this book. It means that you are at a very serious place in your life, and you need change. If you are not at that serious space and you took up this book just out of curiosity, prepare to be transformed!

This book will empower you to prioritize your well-being unapologetically and remind you that self-care is not selfish, but rather an essential foundation for a fulfilling and purpose-driven life. It is packed with actionable strategies on how to take care of, invest in and empower one's self as you explore the multifaceted dimensions of self-care.

This book is more than just a guide—it is a roadmap to living authentically, boldly, and unapologetically. It is a call to reclaim your life and prioritize your self-care journey. So, if you are ready to embark on a riveting adventure of self-discovery, personal transformation, and a life filled with purpose and joy, then "Stop Chasing, Start Living" is the guide you've been waiting for. Happy Reading!

PART A

Chapter 1
The Journey to Self-Transformation

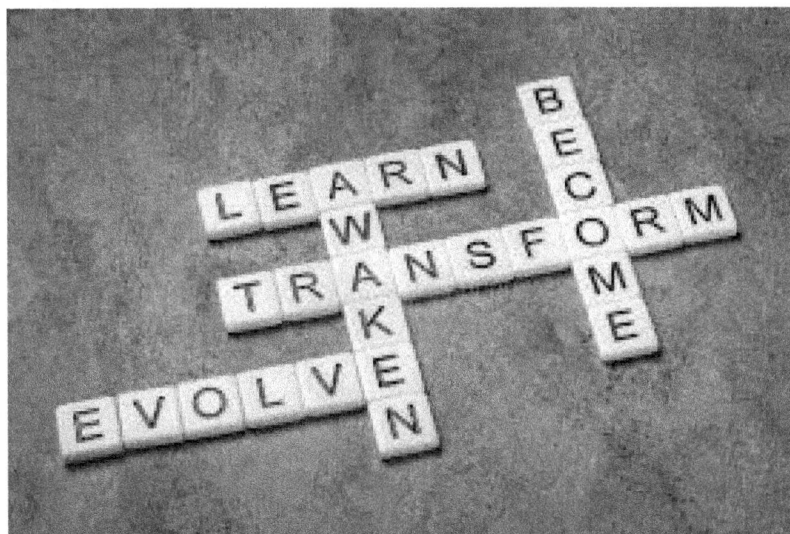

Stop Chasing

Chasing is an act of pursuing something or someone. Chasing implies going quickly or an eager attempt to do something. Attempting to do anything from a place of eagerness may not produce the best results. Whenever we chase after something, we take ourselves out of the present moment where life actually happens; the future doesn't exist yet, and the past is gone. The only meaningful place to live is in the now, and that is generally where you will find what you are looking for.

We are always chasing after something. Which would you say identifies with your current reality?

1. I am chasing the dream (job, man, woman, marriage).
2. I am chasing society's view of an ideal family.
3. I am chasing money.
4. I am chasing security.
5. I am chasing material things.
6. I am chasing youth.
7. I am chasing approval.
8. I am chasing love.
9. I am chasing happiness.
10. I am chasing the path to success.
11. I am chasing the latest trend.

12. I am chasing outer beauty.
13. I am chasing people.

Let us agree on something; there is nothing wrong with desiring the finer things of this life and working hard to acquire them. It is important to remain diligent and persistent in the accomplishment of your goals, dreams, and desires. So, one would ask, how do you know when it becomes a chase? The act of chasing and the act of persistently pursuing one's goals come from two different mindsets. Either is seen when you examine the internal place from which the individual's action is taken.

When you chase something, it is coming from a position of desperation, weakness, anxiety, and neediness. You can end up in a state of panic, fear, uncertainty, and confusion. Persistence, on the other hand, comes from a position of strength and empowerment. Therefore, let us not become confused about the two. You do not want to be chasing anything in this life. The end result of chasing is emptiness. When you make a decision that you want something or that you want to get something done, ask yourself, "Why do I want this? Why do I want this job? This relationship? To start this particular line of business?" Without staying true to your why, you will get the result, but you are not in a state of peace or joy. When you achieve without peace and joy, check if you are aligned with your why.

Start Living

To live means to be in a conscious state of rest and remaining in true purpose. Imagine living a life where you are in a constant place of peace and joy. A life where, no matter the situation, you are not bombarded by fear, tenseness or anxiety. To be in a space of rest means to be in total control of your emotional state, and you take the matter of self-care seriously.

Are you living or merely existing? Are you handling your day-to-day affairs well, in a state of structure and order? "Living" is not reserved for a certain class of people; it is not reserved for the wealthy or the famous. The simple act of peaceful progress toward the accomplishment of your purpose is the art of living. Be mindful of what is stealing that peaceful progress, and practice the self-care routines that will keep you alive to live your best life.

I love to talk about "PEACEFUL PROGRESS" because the opposite of that is "POP-DOWN PROGRESS." Yes, this is a term that Ellecia has coined to express the severity of this kind of progress. Many will work morning, noon, and night without taking a break and getting enough sleep. Rest assured, you will enjoy pop-down progress.

Many will be so busy on the go that they find no time to prepare their own meals at home. They find themselves in the fast lane of the slow drive-through lines picking up junk food in the name of not finding the time to cook. Rest assured, you will enjoy pop-down progress. Pop-down progress is burnt-out progress. You are actively achieving your goals; however, it is being done in a toxic way. Most individuals are living in this state of pop-down progress. They are the individuals who are still in the 9-5 that is creating grief in their minds daily. They are the individuals who are chasing the promotion by drinking coffee at 5 pm to work up until 9 pm at the office. They are the individuals who are not resting well because they take the work home and burn the midnight oil to complete the project, and they are the individuals who eat junk food daily. These lifestyle behaviours will place you in a pop-down state after a while. Come on, what sense does it make for you to chase the progress that will leave you oppressed, sick, and burnt-out. Is it really worth it?

Grounded in Self-Management

Grounded in self is the ability to Take Care Of, Invest in, and Empower Yourself. Grounded in self does NOT mean selfishness. Your first responsibility is to yourself, but that does not mean you should live a selfish life. It means having the wisdom to know that you have a responsibility to take care of yourself so you can live to manifest your God-given purpose. You see, you must first hold yourself accountable before you can point the finger at someone else. You must first be able to keep the commitments that you have made to yourself before you can commit to someone or commit to getting something done for someone. Self-management is your ability to regulate your own behaviors, thoughts, and emotions in a way that better serves you. Since proper self-care is really about managing the whole person (mind, body, and spirit), then one's ability to manage self becomes intrinsic to the execution of proper self-care.

Your health is your wealth. Mind, body, and spirit means that your wellness does not only come from your physical state but also from your mental health and spiritual state as well. To be really healthy, we have to pay attention to all three aspects. The main concept behind the mind-body-spirit connection is that we are more than just our thoughts. We are also our bodies, our emotions, and our spirituality. All these things combine to give us identity, determine our health, and make us who we are. The physical, mental, and spiritual combine to make us who we wholly are. Our ability to practice self-care in all three areas speaks to proper self-management.

The Self-Transformation Journey to Self-Care

It is part of our natural desire/human nature to want to improve, grow and transform our lives as much as we can. It is an internal drive to experience deeper fulfillment. However, though we have this desire, many find themselves so busy it becomes elusive, and they are left with just a hope of getting there. In their minds, it becomes an unrealistic expectation. Maybe you are one of those people who dreamt of taking the self-transformation journey but you do not know where to start. You have been thinking about transforming your mind, body, and spirit routines to produce the very best versions of yourself, but you have been procrastinating. I am here to tell you that you can do it. Just start by taking one step at a time.

Self-transformation is the act of re-directing, re-shaping, re-shifting, and re-fueling one's energy into being a completely different person. Self-transformation is the key to getting unstuck! Self-transformation does not need to have a dramatic effect. It often means simply opening your mind to something that you had a fixed mindset towards or perhaps learning a new skill or sharpening an old one.

23

It involves seeking expert help, conquering self-doubt, fear of failure or fear of success, to developing a new attitude, adopting a new way of doing things and/or forsaking a deluded belief. In the Self-transformation pot, there are two ingredients that MUST be present: discipline and diligence.

The Self-Transformation Plan

In order to let go of the demands of this world and actually start living, one must have a transformed mindset. You must start to unlearn some of the things you grew up believing. You must make a decision to relinquish that which the subconscious mind wants to hold on to.

Self-transformation is attained through a thorough examination of your:

1. Values
2. Reality map
3. Self-awareness
4. Emotional stability

Examination of your Values: What do you stand for? What are some of the things that you will accept and those that are unacceptable? Take some time and evaluate these things before you move on to the next few pages. This analysis will lead you to writing your

24

self-transformation plan. There must be harmony in the different aspects of your life as you seek to self-transform. Take some time to write down some of your deepest Negotiables and Non-Negotiables.

_____

_____

_____

_____

_____

Review your Reality Map: Take some time to look at how you were brought up. The atmosphere that you grew up in and the way you were conditioned as a child can lead to a distorted or disillusioned view of life that needs to be re-evaluated. The way you grew up may be affecting your current paradigm. What are some of the things that you grew up believing that you are trying to shift your mindset on now that you are an adult?

_____

_____

_____

_____

_____

Ellecia Clarke-Edwards

Self-Awareness: In my first book, Two Kingdom Keys to Success, I explored the significance of self-awareness as one of the important factors in living a Kingdom Life. When one is self-aware, they function from a place of consciousness. When one is self-aware, they become very alert of their negative conditioning and take steps to change them. This includes facing and purging depression, anger, fear, etc., and they begin to operate from a place of wholesomeness. Self-mastery is key as you move to self-transform. What are some of the things you are now aware of that has elevated your mindset?

_____

_____

_____

_____

_____

_____

Emotional Stability: You must develop the ability to rise above all circumstances and situations irrespective of how you feel. Your emotional state will affect the actions that you take. When you have a deep inner consciousness of your reaction to life's circumstances, you will begin to operate from a place of unconditional

26

love. List five times that you allowed your emotions to get the better of you:

_____

_____

_____

_____

_____

Take some time to do your personal Self-Transformation Plan. The plan will draw attention to your present behaviours (which is sometimes not the ideal) and will allow you to do some solid introspection so that you can become the best version of yourself. We are naturally wired to become what we see, hear, and think of predominantly. Therefore, if one is not conscious, they will transform into what society dictates. Over time, you may find yourself adopting to the values, perspectives, and precepts of those around you as you slowly drift away from your personal and deep-rooted beliefs.

The Self-Transformation exercise will challenge you to do some deep soul-searching. As you begin, do not feel dismayed about or shy away from it. As I am writing this book, I see where I need to do this exercise as well.

How are you currently operating/being? Write that down and on the other side of the page, go ahead and write down who you want to become (your ideal self). Examine how you will feel at the end of this exercise. Cheers to getting back to your authentic self!

Self-Transformation Plan

Who am I currently?	Who I want to become (my ideal self)

Is self-transformation realistic, and is it really necessary? It is very difficult for one to change from their personal belief system, personal biases, fears, and reactions. There is a constant tug-a-war between the person that you are currently and the person you want to become.

Self-transformation is necessary because that is the only way you can accomplish what you were sent here to do. Unless you are transformed into the person you were predestined to become, you will not experience the fullness of your journey here on earth. Do you agree?

How to Achieve Self-Transformation

1. Be Honest with Yourself: Complete the Self-Transformation Exercise above and do continuous check-ins with yourself. Look at where you are in life in these four quadrants: Spiritual, Financial, Physical, and Relationship. You must also take note of your personal development journey. Identify where any changes should be made and take action.

2. Shifting your Mindset: The condition of your mindset will determine your perspective and outcome. You must be willing to get uncomfortable.

3. Create a Vision: Vision keeps things in perspective and is driven by passion. A vision gives us a clear idea of our life.

4. Invest serious time in Personal Development: This is your responsibility. Get that driver's license for your life and get in the driver's seat. Time invested in personal development daily will allow you to master the different areas of your life. Having the vision in place is one thing, but taking consistent daily action is where the challenge lies. Learn a new skill by watching YouTube videos, listening to podcasts, and reading different genres of books.

5. Create an environment conducive to success. Stay away from negative people! I cannot say it enough. Set up a space in your home that will inspire you to work.

6. Enjoy the Process: When you are too rigid, the journey to success becomes depressive and frustrating, especially when things do not work out how you want it. You will be quick to give up if you are not enjoying the process.

What is Self-Care?

The concept of self-care is different in the mind of everyone. Self-care is such a wide topic that it becomes very difficult to assign one definition to it.

- Self-care is the ability to be present to your emotional, mental, physical, and spiritual needs. Self-care is the foundation of healthcare.
- Self-care is about aligning your life with what brings you joy and peace.
- It is choosing to do what energizes and renews you.

If you feel like something is holding you back spiritually, financially, emotionally, or physically, you have to tap into your inner man to discover what is blocking you and clear out the silt that is hindering your growth. Do not hemorrhage away and allow the situation to leave holes in your soul before you realize it. Lack of motivation and feeling disorganized or anxious are sure signs that self-care is lacking. Self-care is a daily choir and should not be adopted as a last resort. For you to regain and reclaim your peace and joy, you must first clear away the mud and free your mind to accept the abundance.

Why is self-care important, you may ask. Let me answer that question with these words: heart disease, cancer,

31

chronic respiratory disease. These are all lifestyle diseases and represent 63% of all annual death worldwide according to the International Self-Care Foundation. These are known as lifestyle diseases because they are acquired based on one's day-to-day habits; negative habits that eventually become chronic. The good news is that these lifestyle diseases can be controlled and prevented through the adoption of a "health is wealth" mindset.

A "Health is Wealth" mindset is when you get that WOW moment in understanding that you cannot accomplish anything without your health. Unfortunately, that moment dawns on a lot of people when it is too late—when they have already developed a debilitating illness and they are in regret mode. A sick person laying down in bed with a chronic health condition is not able to create the type of impact that they want to create in the world. You will be too busy trying to get well. Furthermore, an unhealthy person's capacity to create wealth is limited. So, before you continue reading, take some time to decide on the type of life you really want to live. I can guarantee that you must be in good health to manifest it.

If you align your purpose to self-care, then you will approach the whole matter of self-care differently. Your purpose is what you were sent on earth to accomplish. Once you know what that is, you will jump out of bed every day wanting to do something to pull you closer toward its accomplishment. When you align self-care to that purpose, you will understand that you are not able to accomplish it unless you "feel good." You NEED to "FEEL GOOD" in order to accomplish your purpose. Feeling good means having that spiritual, mental, physical, and emotional alertness and composure to work toward your God-given purpose!

Starting Your Self-Care Journey

Decluttering

One of the first steps that you must take in efficient self-care is to *declutter;* clear your space! Decluttering means to "remove unnecessary items." It does not mean cleaning up; it means clearing out and removing "stuff." It is therefore a form of letting go of things that are no longer serving you. Overcrowded spaces suffocate your spirit, stifle your creativity, weigh you down, clogs your mental channels, creates stagnation, and make you feel "heavy." I am sure you have done some decluttering before, whether it was a closet, garage, or bedroom, and felt the joy that oozes into your spirit upon completion.

First of all, you will feel a sense of accomplishment having completed the task, and it brings a lighter feel.

When I am feeling disorganized, disoriented, or indecisive, it is normally as a result of feeling mentally cramped. For me, when I find myself in that state, it is normally because my life has gotten too cluttered or is out of order. This is true for almost everyone. I would want you to try this; when you feel chaos and confusion in your inner world, try decluttering the external world and see the result. Indeed, your external environment affects and reflects your inner environment. Go ahead and give yourself a high five once you have done your decluttering to invite the new and the blessings to come in.

Breathe: Tap Into Your Energy

If you are constantly in a state of regret, disappointment, frustration, anger, feeling drained and tired, then your energy is blocked. It means that your energy is situation sensitive. It means that you are living in happiness and not joy. There is a difference between joy and happiness. Joy is of the soul and is an inner feeling. Joy is a fruit of the Spirit (see Galatians 5:22), and when we find joy, it is infused in comfort, wrapped up in peace, and is not based on situations, time, and seasons. Happiness, on the other hand, is fickle. It can be present for weeks and disappear in an instant. Happiness is merely external, fleeting, and is only achievable on earth. Are you experiencing joy or happiness in your life daily?

The individual operating from a conscious state is in search of joy over happiness and are true to themselves by honoring their needs, desires, and boundaries. Being true to yourself means making some tough decisions, like saying no when you are unable to do something, and even deciding to resign from your job that you do not like. When was the last time someone called to pray for you? When was the last time someone genuinely asked you the question "How are you?" and actually wait for a genuine response and not the cliché "I'm okay?" Take notice; your circle is always ready to ask for prayers and unload their problems. These patterns of behavior can eventually drain your energy.

Having more joy in your life requires that you first do an inventory of the content and substance of your life, particularly of your interpersonal relationships, to assess how you are using your energy. Take this test to see where you are on the breathing scale:

1. You feel drained or tired all the time.
2. You set goals but rarely achieve them.
3. Procrastination is now your norm.
4. Your thoughts are scattered, and you are unable to focus.

5. You feel it is mandatory to always please others.
6. It is difficult for you to sit and do nothing.
7. You feel unappreciated in your home, among friends, or at work.

These are signs that your energy is over-extended in other people and things and is not being re-fueled. It also means you are giving away too much of your energy, and there is no reciprocity. You can help and support others but do not act like a superhuman by going around adopting everybody's problems. In managing your energy, you will find that you have more vitality, you have more physical, spiritual, and emotional energy, and you will think more clearly, be more decisive and less defensive.

So now that we have spoken about these two big words: JOY AND HAPPINESS, I have a journaling exercise for you. The question you are answering is "What brings me joy?" It is such a simple question, but it requires deep thoughts to respond. In answering this question, you will once again connect with what nurtures and renews your spirit and feeds your soul. For me, one of the things that renews me spiritually is writing. Writing allows me to think deep, pray more, and activates an awesome creative energy. It brings such joy because I see it as my ministry, and I know that thousands of people will be reading my books as they go on their own self-transformation journey. I also like to read, go out in nature, and travel to new places. I therefore make time to get these things in.

I would love for you to pause in the reading of this book, grab a pen, your journal or simply jot down your thoughts in this book and answer this question "What brings me joy?" Note, I did not ask what makes you happy. If you feel stuck, think back to when you were growing up, probably in your teens: It certainly would represent a different time and season, but sometimes we have to get back to our foundation/roots.

I find JOY in:

1. _____

2. _____

3. _____

4. _____

5. _____

6. _____

7. _____

8. _____

9. _____

10._____

Knowing Who You Are!

It is important for us to walk this life in our own authentic shoes and not someone else's. You may be on the hunt for a shoe that society would want to fit you into, but that shoe will carry you down a road of destruction. Self-mastery is key; your strengths and weaknesses are completely different from another person. The key thing to understand though is that there is no comparison, but you, the individual, must know what those strengths and weaknesses are. The journey that this book intends to take you on is one of self-discovery, self-examination, self-mastering, and self-management. You see, we do not take enough time to understand ourselves. I do believe that it is high time that we start.

I shared in my first book that my self-transformation journey started in 2017 when I travelled to the United States of America. The Lord had to pull me away from everything that I was familiar with to be with Him. This came as a result of me going into fasting and praying in search of more; more than the regular mundane life that

I was living. It was at that time I became conscious of who I am in God.

What is it that is hindering you from walking in your identity? Do you know how powerful you are? Do you realize how much you have inside of you to give? Sometimes we shy away from our greatness because we do not understand how great we are. Telling yourself each day how unique and wonderful you are is you affirming who you are in God. His Word describes us as "chosen people, a royal priesthood, a holy nation…" (see 1 Peter 2:9). I don't know about you, but that sounds like I am quite SPECIAL; of much importance indeed!

When you come into this understanding, you start to walk differently, talk differently, and see the world differently. You will essentially adopt a Kingdom Mindset. This happened to me during my transformation year. How did I get there? I started to read the WORD more. As I continued, I finally started to understand the promises of God and that every one of them applied to me. I finally understood that I could be whomever I wanted to be and accomplish whatever I wanted to accomplish. His Word promises us that "… he is able to do exceedingly abundantly above all that we ask or think…" (see Ephesians 3:20). This brings excitement to my soul each time I read it. It is therefore

Ellecia Clarke-Edwards

important to know and understand who you are in God so you can ultimately walk in your PURPOSE! You can walk in AUTHORITY!

Knowing who you are in God also changes the beliefs that you have of yourself. It is okay to walk into a store and buy an expensive dress for yourself. It is okay to book yourself into an expensive hotel for a few days and just chillax. Many find it difficult to do things of that nature for themselves because they believe they do not deserve it. You have the ability to transform your life, and you deserve to be pampered.

Chapter 2
Taking Care of Self

Love Yourself First

Matthew 22:39 says "...Thou shalt love thy neighbor as thyself." (KJV). This seems like a very simple and practical instruction, but why is it so difficult to execute? This means that you cannot give love if you don't have love within you to give and have it first for yourself. Loving yourself means embracing and accepting yourself, caring for yourself, and honouring who you are in God.

Do you know what your own needs are? An emotionally unstable person cannot aid anyone with emotional issues. Equally, a financially deficient person cannot help the hungry, homeless man on the road to find food and shelter. Repeat after me, "I can only attend to the needs of others when I empower myself and my cup is full. I cannot pour from an empty vessel." Repeat this on a daily basis, and it will prove to be a reminder to yourself that you need to attend to "You" first.

Looking yourself in the mirror daily to own up to your own issues/weaknesses as an individual will do both you and others myriads of good. Being able to do that means that you are operating from a place of maturity and power. Let me clarify any ambiguities that may exist in your mind. This book is by no means perpetuating selfishness. I am not saying you should neglect the needs of others and only attend to your needs. What I am saying is that you should *"Mind your own business (take care of you) before you mind the business of others."* What I am also saying is that you must operate from a genuine place in helping others; do not be a hypocrite. Do not appear to be well in an area that you know you are struggling with. For example, if you have a total lack of control over your spending habits, do not hold a conference on how to manage financial matters. This is a lack of authenticity. In fact, you need to go in search of a conference to attend so you can learn about money matters and money management. Take some time for you—grow and develop yourself in an area before you seek to give a lecture on it.

Heal From the Root: Stop Cutting the Branches

As I stood in front of the mirror one Sunday morning, perming my hair, I heard the voice of the Lord speaking to me. He said, "Address the root before I can release you into greater." So, there I was, peacefully doing my hair and wondering what the Lord was talking about (smile). Naturally, I went into reflection mode.

I started to examine the fact that I had just gone out on the road earlier to purchase a box of hair relaxer to perm my own hair. You see, this is something I have done for years; run to the store to purchase items to get my hair, manicure, and pedicure done. Whenever someone gave me a compliment on my hair and nails, I would say "...and you know I did them myself." Of course, they would look in amazement. Some will say, "I wish I could do that," and I would feed myself this self-aggrandizing line like, "Girl, you so talented." (smile).

As I continued to reflect on my "talent" of doing things for myself, a revelation hit me upside my head. I realized that there was a root cause to it all. You see, before I got married, I was working at the bank, and my salary was spread in many different directions. I had a very tight budget, so I started to look at the areas that I could cut, and it was then that I realized I started to cut the things I claimed I could have done for myself (my hair, manicure and pedicure, facial, etc.). As I was standing and looking in the mirror, watching myself perm my hair, I realized that I was doing my own hair because of a mindset shift that took place many years ago. WOW! It dawned on me that going out to buy the items to do my hair and nails became a robotic type of action, not realizing that I had the capacity to go get these self-care pampering activities done. Can you believe that while I was doing these things, I had the money to go out and get it done? You see, I had managed to convince myself that the reason I am doing these things for myself is because "No one can do it as

44

well as I do." Can you believe that I failed to identify the root cause of a matter that lingered for years? The root belief was lack and scarcity, and that was where I continued to operate from.

What is the point that I am making here: it is not that I am not grateful and happy that I have the capacity to do these things for myself. In fact, I am happy that I was able to save some money while I perfected the art of doing them. Dear Reader, if you are in a season where you have more pressing matters to take care of (like paying off a mountain of debt), then definitely start looking at what you can get done on your own without incurring a lot of expenses. It is great to do something for yourself, especially if you have a financial goal that you want to meet.

Now that that point is made clear, the other point is that there was a need for me to tackle the root cause of my behaviour. The Holy Spirit wanted me to understand that I had shifted my mindset from the necessity of pampering, and I needed to address it. I did not go in pursuit of learning how to do my hair and nails for myself because I had a burning desire to learn something new, but on the contrary, I had managed to convince myself that I could not afford to do it. While that was true based on the season I was in, the belief was so well written in my sub-conscious mind that I failed

Ellecia Clarke-Edwards

to realize that I came out of that season a long time ago. Be very self-aware and learn to discern your season. Do the things you want to do on your own, yes, go right ahead but always remember that self-pampering is necessary. Take yourself out, go get your nails and hair done, go on a vacation. Do it because you deserve it!

Is there something that you are doing, and you have failed to ask yourself "Why am I doing this?" Have you taken the time to examine the root reason for you doing what you are doing? There are times when you must step back and look at the situation that you are going through. You must analyze what is the root cause of your thinking and actions. Once you have discerned that, you have to now start applying the cure to the root and stop cutting the branches.

The other point I am making is one that I have already made somewhere in this book. We put our self-care at the bottom of the list, for some reason or another. For me, it was because I told myself I could not afford it. For someone else, it could be because your parents told you "Money don't grow on trees. Save every dollar." It could be because you have been or are being emotionally, physically, or mentally abused in a relationship by a spouse. Whatever the narrative is that you fed yourself or someone fed you, I want you to own up to it and start questioning yourself. Do not cut the branches off the trees (mountains) in your life; identify the foundation/root cause for your behaviour. Do not be so quick to point out the flaws in others and conveniently sweep yours under the mat.

The Lord said, "Address the root cause so I can release you into greater." In other words "Fix your mindset, girl" (smile). As I thought about the financial aspect of my life and how I was robbing myself of my pampering self-care needs, I started to examine other areas that needed fixing. I jumped over to the physical aspect and immediately started to examine my eating habits. Of course, for many of us, there is always something to fix in this area. In that moment, I made some commitments to myself concerning what I was putting in my mouth. How many times have we heard it, "you are what you eat"? I decided then and there to lessen my meat intake, my sweet intake and to get more consistent with my exercise routine. The results were quite evident as I noticed that my energy level increased and I was getting more restful sleep. Yes, I was definitely dissecting well what the Lord meant when He said "fix the root."

As I continued this self-probe, I made a commitment to myself to make a concerted effort to go to the hairdresser and to trust someone other than myself to do my manicure and pedicure. I wanted to do this, not because I don't like doing it myself, but to erase the belief that I had written in my subconscious mind many years ago that I could not afford it. I encourage you to carry out this exercise, let's "fix ourselves so that we can be released into the greater."

Serving to be Seen

Serving others can promote satisfaction with life, give your life greater meaning, and promote the development of other positive character strengths that enhance the quality of your life and relationships. However, if helping others is done with some selfish motive, such as the need to be liked or to be looked upon as a hero, then life will reward you accordingly. Serving others to be seen is a selfish act that is done to satisfy your own ego.

When you feel compelled to do something for someone else, ask yourself the reason for it. Is it because you are led by the Spirit of God to do so, or is it because you desire to be seen as a good person in the eyes of your peers? Could it be that you are consistently putting the needs of others ahead of yours because there is an innate desire to feel needed? You want to feel like the superhero appearing on a white horse ready to save the day. You put others needs ahead of yours because you want to always be the go-to person, the one who is deemed the smartest. That way, your peers will look at you in admiration, and the praises will put you on high.

48

Ultimately, this will bring such a gratifying feeling and you do not want anyone to take that place.

The point I am making is that you should always examine your motive, reasons, and intentions. Serve because you believe you are called to serve and not because you desire to be praised by man. Constantly neglecting your own needs and serving with the wrong motive in the name of assisting others puts you in a "need for approval" state, and your action will not yield the best result.

Three Tenets of Basic Self-Care (Think Well, Eat Well, Rest Well)

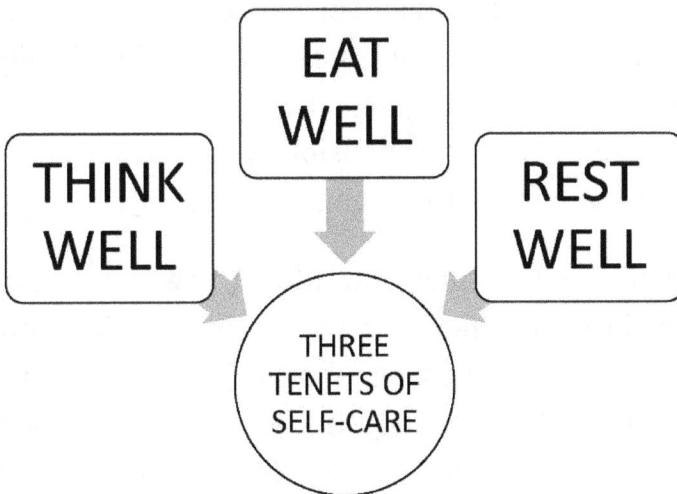

EAT
WELL

THINK
WELL

REST
WELL

THREE
TENETS OF
SELF-CARE

Thinking Well, Eating Well, and Resting Well are the foundational practices of self-care. It is a full-time job that requires attention and responsiveness, and it is certainly an ongoing investment in self.

Tenet #1 - Think Well

To "Think Well" in a general sense means to think positively and remain conscious of the content of your mind. Thinking well must therefore become an intentional and deliberate effort. Your mind impacts your thoughts, behaviours, and emotions and is linked to your overall attitude and outlook on life. It also helps you adapt to the changes in your life so you can cope with it. When you have a healthy, stable mind, you get to do things more productively and effectively. A sound mind stabilizes our entire inner world. The quality of your thoughts determines the quality of your life. Therefore, it is your responsibility to monitor how you feel by keeping your thoughts in check.

Do you want to change your life? A new life starts with a shift in your mindset. If you desire a radical shift in your life, you must change the way you use your mind. You cannot think both negative and positive thoughts at the same time, as one will always dominate the other. As humans, we are creatures of habit, and so are our minds. We must make sure empowering thoughts and positive emotions are the dominating influence in the mind.

An important point that many seem to forget is that in order to manifest external change, internal work must first be done. Trying to change external conditions by working directly on those conditions will almost always prove futile or temporary unless it is accompanied by a change of thoughts and beliefs. Train your conscious mind to think thoughts of success, happiness, health, and prosperity. Learn to weed out negativity, such as fear and worry. Keep your conscious mind busy with the expectation of the best, and make sure the thoughts you habitually think are based upon what you want in your life.

Your thoughts affect what happens to you. Most of us go through life taking little notice of our thought processes: how the mind thinks, what it fears, what it heeds, what it says to itself, and what it brushes aside. For the most part, we go about our lives with minimal attention paid to how we think. We go through life neglecting one of the most important and powerful forces in our life: our thoughts. Remember, what you focus on, you attract.

Tenet #2 - Eat Well

Food is consumed to maintain life and growth. However, the same food, if not consumed in the right form, quantity, and timeframe, can allow you to develop chronic diseases and send you to an early grave.

If you take poison into your body daily in the form of junk food, your body will certainly deteriorate over time. The truth is, our bodies are fighting to stay alive. As human beings, we were uniquely made to dispel waste and toxins from our bodies through natural means. However, there comes a time when your body can do so much and no more. It starts to scream at you by showing little signs here and there as hints that you need to shift your mindset on your eating habits. Eating well means *to eat with a purpose*. This means you will eat what is necessary to pull proper nutrients and not just eating to feel full. You will notice that the "Fillers" that are added to junk food will make you feel full but there really is no nutritional value. Fillers are additives that help to bulk up the weight of the food that we eat so the cost can be lowered.

Some may say that it is expensive to eat healthily, but I would like to challenge that. Have you ever thought of how much money the average person spends on eating out or buying snacks?

When discussing the cost of healthy eating, it is important to consider the cost of not incorporating nutritious foods into meals on a regular basis. Unhealthy dietary patterns that consist of high amounts of sugar, saturated fat, sodium, and calories are linked to higher rates of chronic diseases such as overweight and obesity, heart disease, high blood pressure, and type 2 diabetes, among many others. Not only is the risk of chronic disease greater, but the financial cost of treating the diseases listed is expensive. This therefore indicates that the cost of regularly incorporating nutritious foods into one's diet is much less expensive than the cost of treating chronic diseases later on.

We are what we eat; we are what we think!

The Food Industry

The food industry is a multi-billion-dollar industry. It was not until I started to write this book that I realized how serious it is. Undoubtedly, our body is a complex machine. The food we eat gives our bodies the nutrition and minerals it needs to function properly. What we put into our mouth will determine how our organs function and, ultimately, how long we live. Praying to have good health and long life is futile if you are not eating well.

"Let your food be your medicine and your medicine be your food!" "Eat to Live and do not Live to Eat!" I am

53

sure you have heard these two statements before. As I did research to complete this book, I realized that the food industry's definition of producing food that is geared toward a healthy lifestyle is questionable. Therefore, it is your responsibility to study the labels of the food you are eating and start to pick, choose and refuse at the supermarket. Have you ever studied the labels of the food you are taking into your body on a daily basis? I am challenging you to start examining the packages of the food you consume to see your salt and sugar intake. While I am not a health expert, I have studied enough to know that too much salt, sugar, and oil consumed over time is a death sentence.

If one expects to be transformed and empowered from a self-care prospective, you must invest time to acquire the knowledge to act from an informed position. Looking around, one can say that we are consistently being bombarded to settle where self-care is concerned. The reality is that when you turn on the television, every other advertisement glamorizes fast food and quick lunches. Commercials will illustrate someone biting into a big piece of fried chicken leg or someone sitting on a couch eating salty, sugary, and oily snacks. The reality is that there are fast food restaurants every two minutes or less away from each other. This will certainly have an effect on the mind, allowing you to think that you have no choice but to work with the system. The reality is that when you go to the supermarket, there is an uneven distribution of healthy to unhealthy items. If one is not deliberate and intentional about their health and self-care goals, you will fall in the glamorized world of junk food, which will drive you into becoming a "junkie," yes, a junk food addict. Whether you want to believe it or not, the very television that sits in your living room or bedroom is a tool that is contributing to how we eat and live our lives daily.

I Am Confused About What to Eat

When it comes to nutrition, why are there so many mixed messages? Is the world of nutritional science in a permanent state of turmoil, with no consensus on which foods are good for us? I don't know about you, but I feel confused sometimes about what is considered nutritional food and what is not. I have watched several YouTube videos and done a lot of research on different food kinds; what is good for your body, and what is arsenic. The conclusion that I have drawn is that there is much confusion. Consider this, you have been eating a particular type of food since you were a child thinking that it was good for you, now you are an adult and realize that the "experts" are saying otherwise.

The public is bombarded with information, and it is hard to tell which is true, which is false, and which is merely exaggerated. Foods are sold without clarity about the nutritional content or harmful effects. Each week, a new scientific study is announced telling us the next "new discovery" on which foods will keep us thriving until old age and which foods will put us at risk of developing non-communicable diseases like type-2 diabetes, cardiovascular disease, and obesity. The issue is that often, these studies contradict each other. Should I reduce my dairy intake? Is red meat healthy? Will plant-based foods improve my gum health?

God has designed our bodies in such a unique way that it fights on our behalf to dispel what is harmful and toxic. You must take the bull by the horn and begin to study your own body to know what works for you as an individual. We love our doctors—God bless them—but we can monitor our intake and live long productive lives without ever going to a doctor. Please note that I am not telling you to throw away your doctor's business card and to stay home if you have a serious illness that requires an expert. I am saying take responsibility for your own health and wellness!

Challenge yourself to do some research about the different foods and drinks that you take into your body daily; study the labels and study the ingredients. Some may say, "Look, that is too much work. Eat in moderation, and all shall be well." Guess what, you can be moderately killing yourself (in slow motion). Say no to "moderation" and yes to intentionality. If the food is not good for you, be disciplined - DO NOT EAT IT!

Note that this section of the book is for the reader who has uncovered their purpose and wants to live a long life. If you have a purpose, family, and friends that you love, you must take action now to live long enough to manifest that which God has sent you here to do. Yes, we will die someday, but why contribute to your own death by the things you eat and the way you think? Why shorten your own lifespan and then have "gone too soon" written on your tombstone?

The fact of the matter is, you will not become transformed in the area of self-care if you are not prepared to do your own research and start holding yourself accountable to healthy eating habits.

Solution to the Food Confusion

Solution # 1: Whole vs Processed Food

The key thing to remember when eating is to stick to whole foods and minimally processed, plant-based foods (vegetables, fruits, whole grains, beans, lentils, nuts, and seeds, with water to drink).

We must stop eating processed food! Processed food carries high levels of added sugars, sodium, saturated fats, and refined carbohydrates. Research has connected these nutrients to increased risk and prevalence of obesity and other chronic, nutrition-related diseases. Substantial evidence shows that consuming too much sugar increases risks for type 2 diabetes, heart disease, liver and kidney damage, and some cancers. Personally, I have found that food prepping helps. Similarly to planning what you will do the day before, you should plan your meals a day ahead. The key is to know what you are going to eat or want to eat before you get hungry. This way you can plan and even prepare what you can before the rush of the day. For example, if you decide you will be cooking organic chicken tomorrow, start prepping from the night before by seasoning the chicken and store it in the refrigerator. When you awake, you can start it right away, and that will save you some time. When you wait until you are hungry to eat, you will grab anything to fill that hunger pain and, most of the time, because you did not meal-prep, you will grab junk food.

Solution #2: Front-of-Package Labeling

Another solution to the confusion of eating well is to have front-of-package labelling. Warning labels work by helping consumers identify unhealthy products and discouraging them from consuming these products. Warning labels are better able to help consumers correctly identify products with high content of unhealthy nutrients. Front-of-package warning labels may also encourage manufacturers to improve the nutritional qualities of their products in order to meet nutrition criteria to avoid carrying negative front-of-package labels. It should be mandatory for food manufacturers to practice clear and simple labelling. Transparency about the contents of a product allows consumers to make informed decisions about the food they buy.

It is also the obligation of our leaders and manufacturers to provide healthy options that we can actually believe that nutritional contents on a product is actually what they say it is. While this is necessary to be done, if you are like me, you will take 100% responsibility for your health journey and do your own studies and research.

What is Emotional Eating?

We don't always eat to satisfy physical hunger; we also eat based on our emotions. Emotional eating is one of the number one causes of obesity. The emotional eater uses food for comfort and relieving stress. This individual also uses food to reward themselves; however, this is normally junk food, sweets, and other

Ellecia Clarke-Edwards

unhealthy foods. For the emotional eater, eating is their primary emotional coping mechanism. Their first impulse is to open the refrigerator whenever they are stressed, upset, angry, lonely, exhausted, or bored, and they become stuck in a ridiculously unhealthy cycle where the real feeling or problem is never addressed. It must be noted that emotional hunger is different from physical hunger.

Emotional vs. Physical Hunger

Emotional hunger often creates a zombie-like feeling toward food. Before you know it, you have mindlessly eaten a whole bag of chips or an entire pint of ice cream without really paying attention or fully enjoying it. When you are eating in response to physical hunger, you are typically more aware of what you are doing.

Emotional hunger is like a sudden attack. It comes as an overwhelming and urgent feeling that must be satisfied instantly. Physical hunger, on the other hand, does not demand instant satisfaction and comes on more gradually. The urge to eat doesn't feel as dire (unless you haven't eaten for a very long time).

Emotional hunger craves the stuffed feel. You keep wanting more and more, and the desire is not satisfied, so even though you are full, you eat until you are uncomfortably stuffed. Physical hunger, on the other

60

hand, doesn't need to be stuffed. You feel satisfied when your stomach is full.

Emotional hunger craves specific comfort food. When you are physically hungry, almost anything sounds good—including healthy stuff like vegetables. But emotional hunger craves junk food or sugary snacks that provide an instant rush. You feel like you *need* ice cream or pizza, and nothing else will do.

Emotional hunger is located in the head, not the stomach. An emotional eater's hunger does not come from the stomach; you feel your hunger as a craving you can't get out of your head. You are focused on specific textures, tastes, and smells. The eater feels like they are living to eat and not eating to live.

Emotional hunger often leads to a feeling of shame, guilt, and lack of self-control. When you eat to satisfy physical hunger, you are unlikely to feel guilty or ashamed because you are simply giving your body what it needs. If you feel guilty after you eat, it is likely because you know deep down that you are not eating for nutritional reasons.

Common Causes of Emotional Eating

There is always a deep-rooted cause for your action, and if you sit down long enough to question yourself, you

61

will find the answer. Many times, we cut the branches and do not heal from the root. Healing from the root means identifying the source of the problem and seeking to address it from there. What is the real reason behind the lack of diligence in your self-care routine? Since we are on the topic of emotional eating, let us look at some of the deep causes of emotional eating:

Childhood Habits

One of the common causes of engaging in unhealthy eating is how we were socialized growing up. Think back to your reward system for good behaviour or getting a good report card. The reward is normally going for pizza or having ice cream. These habits can often carry over into adulthood.

Stress

The more uncontrolled stress you have in your life, the more likely you are to turn to food for emotional relief. Ever notice how stress makes you hungry? It is not just in your mind. When stress is chronic—as it so often is in our chaotic, fast-paced world—your body produces high levels of the stress hormone, cortisol. Cortisol triggers cravings for salty, sweet, and fried foods—foods that give you a burst of energy and pleasure.

Stuffing Emotions

Eating can be a way to temporarily silence or "stuff down" uncomfortable emotions, including anger, fear, sadness, anxiety, loneliness, resentment, and shame. While you are numbing yourself with food, you can avoid the difficult emotions you would rather not feel.

Feeling of Loneliness or Emptiness

Do you ever eat simply to give yourself something to do, to relieve boredom, or to fill a void in your life? You feel unfulfilled and empty, and food is a way to occupy your mouth and your time. In the moment, it fills you up and distracts you from the underlying feelings of purposelessness and dissatisfaction with your life.

Social Influences

Getting together with other people for a meal is a great way to relieve stress, but it can also lead to overeating. It is easy to overindulge simply because the food is there or because everyone else is eating. You may also overeat in social situations out of nervousness, or perhaps your family or circle of friends encourages you to overeat, and it is easier to go along with the group.

Which have you identified as your reason for overeating? The primary way to take care of yourself is to have discipline over what you put in your mouth. Like I said earlier in the book, if you link self-care with your purpose, you will start adopting the belief that "I have a responsibility to live long to carry out my purpose." You will begin to hold yourself accountable for what you eat.

Emotional Eating Check

Probably you have been emotionally eating for years and you just don't know. Take some time and test your emotional eating temperature.

- Does food make you feel safe?
- Do you feel like food is a friend?
- Do you regularly reward yourself with food?
- Do you eat more when you are feeling stressed?
- Do you eat when you are not hungry or when you are full?
- Do you eat to feel better (to calm and soothe yourself when you are sad, mad, bored, anxious, etc.)?
- Do you regularly eat until you have stuffed yourself?
- Do you feel powerless or out of control around food?

The first step to change is acknowledgment. You must first admit that there is a problem before you can address the issue. You must face it to fix it. Read the questions again, and from an honest place, make a conscious decision to change. For me, I see where I needed to make some changes myself. Remember, there is nothing to feel bad about; we are all a work in progress while we strive to become our best selves.

The Solution to Emotional Eating

Step 1: Identify your personal triggers.

The first step in putting a stop to emotional eating is identifying your personal triggers. What situations, places, or feelings make you reach for the comfort of food? Most emotional eating is linked to unpleasant feelings, but it can also be triggered by positive emotions, such as rewarding yourself for achieving a goal or celebrating a holiday or happy event. Note that there is nothing wrong with celebrating with food and having some comfort food around but be mindful of how much you consume.

Step 2: Stay Alert: Stay Self-Aware

Tarry for five minutes before you give in to the craving. Emotional eating tends to be automatic and virtually mindless. Before you even realize what you are doing, you have reached for a tub of ice cream and polished off half of it. But if you can take a moment to pause and reflect when you are hit with a craving, you give yourself the opportunity to make a different decision.

While you are waiting, check in with yourself. How are you feeling? What is going on emotionally? Even if you end up eating, you will have a better understanding of why you did it. This can help you set yourself up for a different response next time.

Step 3: Find other ways to fulfil yourself emotionally.

If you don't know how to manage your emotions in a way that doesn't involve food, you won't be able to control your eating habits for very long. Diets so often fail because they offer logical nutritional advice, which only works if you have conscious control over your eating habits. It doesn't work when emotions hijack the process, demanding an immediate payoff with food.

When you are physically strong, relaxed, and well rested, you are better able to handle the curveballs that life inevitably throws your way. But when you are already exhausted and overwhelmed, any little hiccup has the potential to send you off the rails and straight toward the refrigerator. Exercise, sleep, and other healthy lifestyle habits will help you get through difficult times without emotional eating. These lifestyle habits will put you in a place of confidence and control over your life. Here are some pointed suggestions:

- **Exercise:** physical activity improves your mood and energy levels, and it is also a powerful stress reducer.

- **Aim for 8 hours of sleep every night.** Lack of sleep causes your body to crave sugary foods that will give you a quick energy boost. Getting plenty of rest will help with appetite control and reduce food cravings.

- **Make time for relaxation.** Give yourself permission to take at least 30 minutes every day to relax, decompress, and unwind. This is your time to take a break from your responsibilities and recharge your batteries.

- **Activate your Social Circle.** Don't underestimate the importance of close relationships and social activities. Spending time with positive people who enhance your life will help protect you from the negative effects of stress.

- **Talk to Your Spouse:** Can you talk to your spouse about anything? If that is not the type of relationship you have with your spouse, then as a couple, sit and have a serious conversation about the matter of expression of emotions.

Step 4: Be realistic. Learn to accept your feelings, even the bad ones.

Do not pretend to be a superhero. You will not always be in a peak state; accept it. Suppressing your feelings will drive you to the refrigerator. This goes back to step 2; remain self-aware and stay connected to your moment-to-moment experience. Do not obsess or stress over your emotions; even the most painful and difficult feelings subside relatively quickly and lose their power to control your attention.

While it may seem that the core problem is that you are powerless over food, emotional eating stems from feeling powerless over your emotions. You don't feel capable of dealing with your feelings head on, so you avoid them with food.

Step 5: Practice Mindful Eating

Indulge without overeating by savouring your food. Slowing down and savouring your food is an important aspect of mindful eating, the opposite of mindless, emotional eating. Try taking a few deep breaths before starting your food, putting your utensils down between bites, and really focusing on the experience of eating. Pay attention to the textures, shapes, colours, and smell of your food. How does each mouthful taste? How does it make your body feel?

By slowing down in this way, you will find that you appreciate each bite of food. You can even indulge in your favourite foods and feel full on much less. It takes time for the body's fullness signal to reach your brain, so taking a few moments to consider how you feel after each bite can help you avoid overeating.

When you eat to feed your feelings, you tend to do so quickly, mindlessly consuming food on autopilot. You eat so fast that you miss out on the different tastes and textures of your food—as well as your body's cues that you are full and no longer hungry. By slowing down and savoring every bite, you will not only enjoy your food more, but you will also be less likely to overeat.

Tenet #3 - Rest Well

Until I started to write this book, I did not understand the significance of sleep. As I went deeper into reading and researching about sleep, I was amazed at the many health benefits that exist. Having a good night's rest is actually critical to proper health and wellness. Before now, I actually thought that four hours of rest nightly was perfectly fine. My reasoning was "Who has time to be sleeping 7 to 8 hours per night anyways, with all the things I have to do." Well now, what can I say, after you finish reading this section of the book, just as how my mind changed, so will yours if you are not big on sleep.

Ellecia Clarke-Edwards

Health Benefits of Sleep

1. **Sleep can Boost Your Immune System.** Getting a good night's sleep can help to keep your immune system fighting and keep germs at bay. Sleep gives your body the time it needs to rest and repair, which is one of the reasons you feel tired and want to sleep more when you are unwell. Sleep supports the proteins and cells of your immune system to detect and destroy any foreign invaders your body might come in contact with, like the common cold. It also helps these cells to remember these invaders, so if you come across the same bugs and germs again, you are prepared to fight them off. So, a good night's sleep helps to strengthen your body's immune response, and it is essential to allow yourself time to rest and recover when you are not feeling well.

2. **Helps to maintain healthy weight gain.** Sleeping will not shed massive pounds from you, but it can help prevent weight gain. When you do not get enough sleep, it increases your stress level, which has the ripple effect of low energy. This will result in you having a low resistance to junk food.

3. **When you sleep, you will find yourself in a better mood.** Being rested helps your energy level to soar. Higher energy means a happier you.

4. **Sleep increases productivity.** Sleep has been linked to higher concentration and higher cognitive function.

5. **Sleep increases exercise performance.**

6. **Sleep improves memory and keeps your heart healthy.**

7. **Sleep leaves you emotionally charged.** If you have a lot on your mind and are struggling with your emotions, going over things in your head can often keep you awake at night. If you are up all night worrying, you might begin to see a change in your mood, and a lack of sleep can leave you feeling low. This could then cause you to feel anxious and create more negative thoughts about not sleeping. This might keep you awake even longer and can turn into a vicious cycle of worry and poor sleep. Try practicing mindfulness to help you sleep and take care of your emotional well-being. Or try putting pen to paper and writing your concerns in a diary before bed. This

could help put your thoughts in order and help you get to sleep.

8. **Sleep keeps you mentally healthy.** Not only is sleep important when looking after your physical health, but it plays an important role in looking after your mental health too. If you are not sleeping properly, you are at a higher risk of developing poor mental health.

9. **Reduce your stress levels.** There are lots of things that can cause you to feel stressed, and how you personally deal with stress will be different from someone else. Feeling stressed, for example, from work, relationships, financial or health concerns, is often a key factor if you are struggling to sleep at night. When you are feeling stressed, your body releases 'stress hormones,' for example, cortisol, which can keep you awake. On the other hand, a good night's sleep can have the opposite effect and relax the systems in your body that are responsible for this stress response.

10. **Maintain good relationships.** It is no secret that a bad night's sleep can leave you feeling grumpy. So, making sure to get enough good sleep can

help to put you in a more positive headspace. When you are feeling good, it is likely to be felt by the people around you, like your colleagues and loved ones. Therefore, getting enough sleep can help you to maintain good interpersonal relationships. Not only that, but how much sleep you get can affect your language, reasoning, and communication skills—all key factors when building relationships with others.

11. **Improve your attention and concentration.** It is no surprise that getting a good night's sleep can help to keep your energy levels up. Plenty of rest can also help to keep your mind from wandering and maintain your attention throughout the day. Not sleeping properly can mean that both your body and brain don't function properly the next day. It could impair your attention span, concentration, strategic thinking, risk assessment, and reaction times. This is even more important if you have a big decision to make, are driving, or are operating heavy machinery. So, getting plenty of sleep can help you to stay sharp and focused all day long.

Self-Awareness and Self-Care

You will take action based on your knowledge of a particular situation or condition, physical or mental. How you speak and what you speak is based on your acquired knowledge. When one has knowledge of something, it represents the basic starting position of a checklist of things to do for future activities. Self-awareness is important because it allows the individual to identify and act on areas that need improvement. For example, someone who knows their body mass index (BMI) will know that once their weight is over a certain number, they are entering the overweight to obese category. A lack of self-awareness plays a part in the slow, incremental loss of health that leads to many non-communicable diseases. No one becomes overweight or develops risk-factors for non-communicable diseases overnight; these problems develop slowly over years of poor self-care and inadequate self-awareness.

How would you rate your health literacy? We know that it is important to measure and monitor health, but how do we do this? A person with good self-awareness of their health would know and have recorded the general metrics that track levels of health and disease. While a large list, in general, you should have some knowledge of your family's medical history and any genetic predispositions, your cholesterol levels, your weight, height, and body mass index (BMI), etc. Once you are aware of the above, you will know how to structure your diet and your daily physical activities.

Listen, you must strive to live a proactive lifestyle and not a reactive one. The three tenets that you just read through represent the basics of self-care. Start every day by monitoring your thoughts; think of what you will be eating from the day before so you can food prep and stick to a sleeping routine. This speaks to your ability to manage yourself well. Proper self-care all boils down to proper self-management.

The "Burnout" Syndrome

To be burnout is a condition of chronic stress. This type of stress comes from mental, physical, and emotional stress, and it is now affecting millions of people. The burnout syndrome arises from the "constant moving syndrome" where life is likened to running on a treadmill. Think about it? How long can one truly run on a treadmill without feeling excess tiredness? Let us examine for a moment how the treadmill works. You get on it, adjust it to the speed that is best for you, and you start running or walking. Let us allude this to the regular pattern of life: waking up, getting the kids ready, making breakfast, going to work, etc. These are daily activities that result in that overwhelming feeling sometimes. When you become tired while walking on a treadmill, you will get off and rest for a while. It is the same way you need to remain in a state of alertness to understand when you need to press the pause button and chillax. You have been going, going, going on the treadmill of life for too long, and you need to stop the treadmill, get off and rest a while. The treadmill of life encompasses all the different areas of our lives which need attention. It is inevitable that you will become over-burdened and stressed if you do not slow down and breathe. Say it with me, "I sometimes need to slow down and breathe."

Being burnout and exhausted is a direct result of the lack of self-focus. This is becoming quite common because most people associate resting with being lazy. If you are sick, exhausted, overworked, overwhelmed, resentful and angry, you cannot be present for those you love. If you are burnout, you will have nothing inside you to give. It is important to focus on your goals but do not obsess over them. Keep your journey productive and fun so you remain motivated. Also, do not overwork your mind by sitting and thinking about your goals 24/7; this will cause burnout. Overthinking can create mental lethargy and stress. Do not beat yourself up for missing a deadline either; things do not always work out as planned, so give yourself some grace.

Your Body is Talking? Are You Listening?

I want you to take this heading very seriously! Your body speaks to you every day. Your body will give you hints when something is wrong; it always does. The problem is that we do not take the time out to notice its language. That language is the little swelling, that sudden pain, the bad feeling, the exhaustion, etc. Anything that is out of the norm is cause for concern and needs attention. Ask your body what it needs to feel better right away, and when it answers, be ready to honor that need.

- If your body is feeling anxious, try this breathing technique. Pull your shoulders all the way up to your ears, then exhale with a whoosh and repeat until you feel calmer.
- If you are hungry, grab a quick healthy snack.
- If you are thirsty, drink some water.
- If you are restless, take a break and go for a short walk.
- If you are achy or stiff, stretch.
- If you are tired, take a nap if you can. If not, try taking a two-minute vacation. Close your eyes and imagine yourself relaxing in a beautiful, peaceful place. Let your worries and exhaustion go for those two minutes while you soak up the feeling of calm relaxation.

All of us are different, so your body will speak to you differently. The tough part is that you must get to know yourself to understand the physiological signals that your body gives.

Tune Into Yourself

To "friend" another nowadays takes the click of a mouse. To be a friend to yourself is a much more difficult task. It means considering your own needs and wants as you engage with the world. It is a delicate balance and a constant negotiation. It is also learned behavior because it is not something we typically learn growing up. If I should ask you, "What strategies do you use to tune into yourself?", would you be able to tell me? Yes, I agree; very interesting question.

Staying in tune with your body also means that you find out what your body needs on a long-term basis to heal and thrive in the future.

- Do you need to go back to the gym?
- Do you need to stop eating at night?
- Do you need to replace your mattress to get a better night's sleep?
- Do you need to ask for help at work or at home?
- Do you need to schedule a massage?
- Do you need to forgive yourself or someone else?

- Do you need to start speaking up for yourself?

Self-care is essential to your well-being and being in the world. When you prioritize self-care, you will show up better and brighter in every other part of your life. When I am having a stressful week, a relationship, or a personal issue, my self-care rituals save the day. In a time when most of us need an alarm and a google calendar to get anything done, self-care rituals are like scheduled personal dates that instantly remind you to check in with yourself. Saying a mantra out loud in bed every morning, unwinding with a prayer before bed, even keeping a vial of essential oils in the car—small practices like these can have a big impact across the board. Put small self-care practices on your calendar. Put anything on your calendar that feeds your soul and nourishes your body. Grant yourself permission to adopt a routine that serves your highest self. Only then can you serve the world.

The unfortunate fact of our modern life is that it is now way easier to tune out than it is to tune in. We live in an external world. Opening up our laptops can feel like stepping into Times Square. Our communities are global, our jobs are 24/7 and the traffic of ideas and images and messages flowing through our system is non-stop. So many external elements are vying for our attention that we are constantly on the look-out, and not looking in. At the end of the day, your biggest responsibility is YOU. Your body is always sending you feedback—so tune in, take notes, and start writing a new rule book for how you will care for yourself starting now. With practice, consistency, and a commitment to listening, you can set up ways of being and thinking that will do wonders for your body and soul.

It is important to stay present and accept pleasure and pain as part of your journey to spiritual health and balance. Your ego naturally leans toward pleasure and comfort. It takes a concerted effort and discipline to begin exploring the truth of who you are and creating a stronger connection to your true self.

Say "No" Gracefully (and Firmly): Cut Hypocrisy

You are doing yourself a grave injustice when you play a hypocrite with yourself and with others. Committing to a request that you did not want to do speaks to your inability to remain true to self. You cannot be everything to everyone. You must learn to say no and say it gracefully and firmly.

Believe it or not, the work you are rushing to finish will not end. There will always be something to do. God created day and night for a reason. Nights are meant for restoration and renewal for you to go again the following day. Your friends, family, and co-workers will always have challenges, and there will always be something urgent that needs to be attended to. However, you must learn to do what you can but do not play God in the life of anyone. It is generally understood that people are afraid to say no because it can be perceived as being rude; you are afraid the person will become disappointed, unhappy or even stop talking to you. Understand this, people will always be who they are. Try giving an unfavourable response after saying "yes" fifty times and see the result. You will be criticized and thrown under the bus for giving an authentic "no." The point is, either way, you will not be liked at some point, so desist from seeking the approval of people by always saying "yes" even when you do not want to.

The clearer you are about who you are and what your vision/purpose is, the easier it is to say no. This is especially true if you know what you are saying no to is not an act of disobedience based on the instructions from the Lord. For example, if you are in a season of your life where solitude is a priority, then going to the movies with friends is not a priority for you. It is very important to discern the season you are in and honour that season. If you are in a season of solitude, the Lord may be calling you into that season to give you divine instructions for your next big season. If you do not honour that time, you may miss what God is trying to

81

say to you and thus miss out on the vastness of your next season. Therefore, you must use your God-given discernment in knowing when to say no gracefully and firmly.

Comfortably Disappoint Others

Do you know those people that try to manipulate you into doing something for them? Come on, we all know those people—those individuals who try to make you feel guilty for denying their request. Like I said earlier, do what is within your capacity to do and leave the rest.

Disappointing others may actually be an appointment for them. I have had to learn that you must consult with the Lord to get the release to be a blessing to others. This is especially true in relation to your finances. I personally believe that we go through processes and seasons of our lives for a reason. The Lord will allow some things to happen to us to teach and mold us into becoming the best version of ourselves. You must consult with the Lord because He may be taking the person that you want to bless financially through a season where they are being taught how to take their faith and patience in Him to another level. If you give without getting that release from the Lord, you are interfering in that person's process; you are interfering in God's transformation process.

When I say that you must get comfortable hurting other's feelings and upsetting others, it simply means that people will be hurt when you deny their request, and they will walk away feeling upset. However, once this is done from a place of love, do not feel guilty. Help if you can, but if you genuinely do not have the capacity to do so, "rest" with your decision; be comfortable with your decision and move on. Do not step out of character or God's instructions to please anyone. If you want to live an authentic, meaningful life, understand that it is not possible to please everyone.

Sometimes I wonder if there is an award that many are vying for—the *"Best 'Yes' Person"* award. That is an award that goes to the person who agrees with all the thoughts, requests, and opinions of the people around them. They crave the love and attention of the crowd so much that they step out of their authentic self to become a professional hypocrite. This is the person that smiles while they are complying with a request and frowns in the person's absence. This section of the book represents a genuine reminder that you should attend to your true self, your needs, speak up for yourself, and do not be a hypocrite. Whether you want to believe it or not, these are self-care activities.

Ellecia Clarke-Edwards

Meditation vs. Medication

Meditation is the art of sitting in quietness to settle your mind. One meditates to create a sense of tranquility and inner harmony that will ultimately achieve a higher sense of self-awareness. Meditation, as used here, is therefore used from a spiritual perspective, which will ultimately lead to a deeper connection and intimacy with the Holy Spirit and to become more self-aware.

I describe it as an art because, in this busy world, it is very difficult to sit in quietness to settle the mind. Indeed, we are constantly busy thinking about the next goal, the next project, and balancing the different areas of our lives. This creates an inner need to be moving all the time. We are now living in a society where it is the norm to speak of how busy we are. We all echo the sentiment of there not being enough time in the day. In fact, "society" will label you as being lazy if you do not see yourself falling into this "busy" category.

There is a craving for man to be in the company of others. However, you need to make time to sit by yourself, in a quiet place, to slow down so you can hear what God is saying. You can be busy doing nothing (lacking results), and therefore slowing down becomes important so you can Rest, Rejuvenate, Re-align, and Re-assess. Taking this time to sit in meditation will

84

allow you to put things into perspective. When you sit to meditate:

- Ensure it is a quiet space.
- Sit comfortably so your body feels relaxed.
- Breathe gently in and out.
- Become aware of the distractions and let them go.

The burnout syndrome, as mentioned earlier, is real. Those who develop this syndrome are people who are consistently on the go. They use energy pills and energy drinks to give them the extra push to outwork work! These are the people who answer the unfortunate hospital calls. This is where the body shuts down and leaves you laying down on your back and forcing you into "meditation" while you are now on "medication" to recover. Meditation is better than medication! If you fail to find the time to meditate and find your center, you are automatically agreeing to the hospital's call. The acquisition of material possessions is fine; everyone wants to live their best life. However, do not chase it, callously neglecting yourself in the midst. Every day you arise from your bed, you have a decision to make: Am I going to chase or mindfully pursue my goals? Am I choosing meditation or medication?

Some of the many health benefits of meditation are:

- Improvement of self-awareness and self-esteem.
- Reduced stress.
- Better focus and concentration.
- Helps to manage anxiety and depression.
- Increase calmness, clarity and promote happiness.

One sure way to create a dependency on medication is to live in regret. To live in regret is to feel sorrow or disappointment for something that happened in the past. Everyone experiences regret in some form; after all, this is life, and we do not always get it right. In the moment of regret, remember that we never make a decision hoping that we will be wrong. Therefore, you must exercise self-compassion. Self-compassion is the highest form of self-care. What is gone is gone; the past is the past; leave it there and move on. You must think solutions. "What is the solution to this regretful scene that I am living in right now? How do I fix this current situation?" Once you activate your mind to find the solution, that is the first step to releasing yourself from the pain of regret.

I encourage you to schedule your meditation time because the cost of medication is regret and a whole lot of money behind it.

CHAPTER 3
INVESTING IN SELF FIRST

You will never be fully happy with what you have, but you will always be happy with the person you have become. Investing in yourself is the biggest gift you can give back to yourself. When you create value around your name, your accomplishments will speak for you. Les Brown said, "Success leaves clues." On a daily basis, you should be doing something that adds value to "YOU" as a person. It can be as simple as learning a new word or as complex as starting your Doctoral Degree. Whichever it is, understand that any form of self-improvement or personal development will draw opportunities and people of excellence to you. You will become like a magnet, pulling individuals of worth that have the capacity to bless you into the next level of your purpose and in the next season of your life.

Personal growth and development/self-improvement is a process of both understanding yourself and pushing yourself to reach your highest potential. It means always asking yourself who you are becoming and how you plan to get there. Essentially, personal development is an investment in your life, and it is a lifelong process.

Investing in personal development will shift you from QUANTITY to QUALITY. Personal development gives meaning, purpose, and direction to your days. It improves your life by helping you deal better with negative experiences too. It is about taking the time and making the commitment to invest in your greatest resource—YOU! Many people are not very interested in personal development because the results are not immediately quantifiable. However, the greatest achievers in life know that the key to success is the ability to manage yourself in a variety of situations. That ability comes through personal development. Personal development requires that you take very deliberate and intentional steps to improve on a daily basis. These include:

1. Knowing what you want to improve and reading books about it.
2. Finding a mentor.
3. Reflecting at the end of each day.
4. Creating a daily success routine.
5. Finding others to empower, motivate and inspire you.
6. Create a reward system.
7. Stay honest with yourself.

Growing into the best version of yourself requires that you work on "you" on a daily basis. Are you willing to pray for yourself? To take those deliberate steps to grow and renew your mind? Remember, in order for a flower to blossom, you must first water the roots. Are you watering the roots of your soul so you can truly blossom into the gem God predestined you to be? You can invest in yourself by:

- Creating a Personal Development Action Plan
- Starting your Own Business.
- Read! Read! Read

Create a Personal Development Action Plan

To successfully create a Personal Development Action Plan (PDAP), you must first be willing to highlight your weaknesses. It is very easy to speak about the things that we are good at, but we sweep the weaknesses under the carpet. What are the areas in your life that you know you need help with? It can be in the area of your emotions; it can be lust; it can be unforgiveness. You must first admit that those weaknesses exist and be willing to fix them. Unfortunately, we have allowed society to dictate to us. Society says that we should portray an image that everything is good all the time. It says that we should post these fancy pictures on our social media pages showcasing how fabulous we are. Yes, we live our lives in seasons; there will be the good season and also the bad. However, if you are in a bad season, don't be afraid to take some time off, look yourself in the mirror and say, "I am not doing well. I am not feeling well. How will I fix this situation that I am going through? How will I heal from this hurtful season of my life?" If you are not willing to accept the flaws—the weaknesses—and be ready to be honest with yourself, you will not be ready to start this Action Plan.

Personal development planning is a structured process that helps create an Action Plan for self-improvement, growth, and development. However, before you can change for the long term, you need to reflect on your current situation. To create an accurate assessment, let us apply the SWOT. In business, SWOT Analysis uncovers the Strengths and Weaknesses of an organization, and identifies the Opportunities and Threats that it faces. SWOT analysis is a framework used to evaluate a company's competitive position and to develop strategic planning. SWOT analysis assesses the internal and external factors as well as current and future potential.

Though the SWOT is a term used in business, it can also be applied to your personal situation. By using it, you can gain a solid understanding of where you are now, and you can think about where you want to go. SWOT may be used as an analysis tool to help you explore areas for change and growth, which can help with goal setting and overall planning. Below are some questions to help you get started.

STRENGTH and OPPORTUNITIES: By knowing your strengths, you can focus your efforts on the things that you are good at. Therefore, taken together, your strengths and opportunities help you identify potential long-term career goals. Write down your answers based on the questions below.

Strengths

1. What do you do best?
2. What unique knowledge, talent or resources do you have?
3. What advantages do you have?
4. What do other people say you do well?
5. What resources do you have available?
6. What is your greatest achievement?

_____

_____

_____

_____

_____

_____

_____

_____

Opportunities

1. How can you turn your strengths into opportunities?
2. How can you turn your weaknesses into opportunities?
3. What could you do today that isn't being done?
4. Who could you support based on your skills?

_____

_____

_____

_____

_____

_____

_____

_____

WEAKNESSES and THREATS: By understanding your weaknesses, you know what to avoid, what to improve, and where you need to get help. Your weaknesses and the threats you face are the things that need to be managed, mitigated, or planned for, to ensure your goals remain achievable. Write down your answers based on the questions below:

Weaknesses

1. What could you improve?
2. What knowledge, talent, skills and/or resources are you lacking?
3. What disadvantages do you have?
4. What do other people say you don't do well?
5. In what areas do you need more training?

_____

_____

_____

_____

_____

_____

_____

_____

Threats

1. What obstacles do you face?
2. Could any of your weaknesses prevent you from meeting your goals?
3. Who or what can cause you problems in the future? How?

4. What are some of the things/conditions that can negatively impact your ability to accomplish your goals?

_____

_____

_____

_____

_____

_____

_____

_____

Going Back to School

Another way to invest in yourself is to go back to school. This does not necessarily mean going into a classroom setting. It can be that you learn a new skill online, download a free course or read books on an area of interest. It is anything you do to learn something new and to increase your knowledge. Your personal development plan should always include what you need to do to become the best version of yourself. In some parts of the world, your credentials do play a role in how quickly you are promoted in an organization. It also determines your level of association and the conference table that you sit around (unfortunately).

In other parts of the world, a University or College level education does not guarantee success or some kind of automatic climb on the corporate ladder. I can unreservedly make that statement because I saw it while I was in Banking. When I started my banking career in 2006, I was shocked to see the number of people who had their master's degree working on the teller line. A college degree also does not guarantee how successful you will become in business. In fact, the majority of the successful individuals that I have studied to date do not have a college or university-level education, for example, Richard Brandon, Steve Jobs, Mark Zuckerberg, etc.

The bottom line is that it is always a good idea to invest in the improvement of your educational level. Going back to school takes an elevated mind, coupled with the big C—Commitment. At the end of the course or program, you will find yourself walking and talking at another level, having acquired another skill. You have procrastinated long enough; NOW is the time to go get that program/course done or completed. NO MORE DELAYS!

Invest Your Time Well

In practicing real self-care, you must eradicate confusion from your life's journey and invest your time well. Time helps us make a good habit of structuring and organizing our daily activities. Time is the most valuable resource because you cannot get it back. Without structure and proper time management, you will feel confused. Confusion stifles creativity and throws you off track with your life's goals. It is the duty of man to preserve time and not to let it go to waste without proper exploitation. The fact is:

- Time acts as both a teacher and a healer. Sometimes, the only way to get a new, healthy outlook on a situation is to give it time. Time teaches us the value of life and makes us feel happy to be alive. A difficult or painful situation will seem less bad as time passes.

- Nobody knows how much time they have. People can die at any age and for any reason.

- Every single thing in the universe is bound to time. Gradually all things start aging and eventually decay as time progresses.

- We are aware of three stages of time: the past, the present, and the future, but the only time we actually have is the present.

- Time affects happiness. A person's perspective of time has a big impact on their happiness and peace of mind.

- Mastering our available time is essential. Managing it poorly or well has a huge impact on life.

- Skill-development takes time, whether that skill is what you love or what you think is best for your future; it depends on how much time you invest.

- Relationships are made or broken due to the amount of time you invest. The amount of time you invest is often the main difference between a deep relationship, loyalty, and one that is shallow.

- Everyone has the same 24 hours a day, so no one can complain about not having time for the things they want to do.

There is a direct correlation between time management and the progress of your growth. How do you spend your 24 hours? When you really start to examine how you spend your day, you will realize that you do have time that you can use to practice proper self-care and personal development.

The ROI of Self-Improvement

Return On Investment (ROI) is a term used in the financial management world. It measures what you get back compared to what you put in. Let me break it down into biblical terms; it means you will reap whatever you sow. As you are reading this book, you are being challenged to take care, empower, and invest in yourself. How much time are you willing to invest to yield the greatest return so you can become the best version of yourself? In other words, you will continue to be mediocre and operate below par if you continue to invest little time in yourself.

Let us look at it from a business perspective. Whenever you invest money or time into your business, you need to have a goal in mind, and the intention is to make a profit. The more time that you invest in your business is the more it reflects in the company's bottom line. What will you gain/profit from taking care of, empowering, and investing in yourself? What result are you looking for? When you look in the mirror, are you satisfied with the person staring back at you? Excellence requires diligence; therefore, the return of investing heavily into yourself is a solid success. The return on investing in yourself is the accomplishment of your purpose.

How will you accomplish your God-given purpose unless you take care of yourself (mind, body, spirit)? Self-care should therefore be seen as an obligation so you can live long enough to accomplish your purpose. Therefore, if you have self-care at the bottom of your to-do list, it is time to take action. If you are serious about what God has purposed for you to do, you will begin prioritizing your self-care plans.

Start Your Own Business

Starting your own business sounds very difficult and may seem like a daunting task. However, this is one way to both invest in and challenge yourself. Why not build a legacy around your name? Why not build a business that your children can inherit? When you take on the venture of starting your own business, you are literally betting on yourself, and you must start with a growth mindset. The decision to start your own business comes with the decision to grow as an individual. It seems daunting to many because it is perceived as difficult and, to some, unachievable. On the contrary, starting your own business is the simple act of doing the thing(s) that you love while earning. What are you good at? Write it down today and ask yourself, how can I monetize this/these gift(s)? Remember, questioning yourself pressures your mind to give you an answer. It may not give you the answer right away but continue to "seek and you shall find."

"What if I am comfortable working my regular 9-5 job? I do not see myself as a business owner." This is also fine; we will not all be entrepreneurs or large business owners. You must live your life from a place of authenticity. If you believe you were not called to manage a business, then play the most excellent role you possibly can, providing support to an organization. Once that decision is made from a place of solid consciousness and truth, then proceed with what makes you happy. This section of the book is for those persons who know for a fact that God has called them into entrepreneurship.

Remember, always operate from a space of boldness. If you really are thinking about starting your own business, do not allow fear to hold you back. Also, do not rationalize either; to think that you cannot have a 9-5 and have a business. You see, we grew up with the belief that we must go to school and get a 9-5 job; therefore, anything outside of that almost seems unacceptable and unachievable. I remember when I decided to invest in myself by starting my own business. I was fearful, and I started to give myself all the reasons why I shouldn't proceed with the decision. I had to work very hard to overcome some well-ingrained self-limiting beliefs. In fact, I became so bold that I started my business while I had a 9-5, until I was able to work my way out of the 9-5.

Let me quickly share how that happened. I always wanted to own a hair, beauty and cosmetic business and I took the bold step to register that business in 2019. I figured let me take baby steps toward my dream of owning my own business while I was in my 9-5 job as a Sales Manager. When I registered the business, it ignited a fire in my belly that was incomprehensible.

I started to do research after work and on weekends and complete the basics such as completing a business plan, opening a social media account and shipping logistics. Yes, you can do all of that while you are in your 9-5. It is called creating a transition plan. I eventually started to sell a few products online.

Fast forward to mid 2020, I had started a new job as a Sales Manager at another company. I was just about to be confirmed on the job when the company decided to make the COVID-19 vaccine a mandatory requirement to remain with the company. To be honest, I was not comfortable with the vaccine, so I took the difficult decision to resign. Note that this was a huge faith move. Though I had support in the form of my husband and other family members, I was still very concerned that I was losing my main source of income. When I handed in the resignation letter and did the exit interview, I drove home talking to the Lord and I felt so much peace. This is how I knew that I made the right decision.

I had continued to do my online business through Instagram from 2019 and had some funds coming in but it was not anything to talk about. I decided once again to make another bold move by searching for a store space. I had noticed that a new plaza was finishing up in the town of the community where I lived and decided to check out the location.

When I went, I saw a gentleman sitting on the step of the first floor of a three-story building. I approached him and asked if he knew if there were any store spaces for rent. He said he was there inquiring about the same thing. We stood there for another thirty minutes just talking about real estate. When the real estate agent came and the gentleman that I met on the step introduced me to her, she said "Go ahead and sign up these documents just in case a shop becomes available." I signed up the documents and I left. When I drove out,

I started to pray and declare that I would acquire one of those shops to start my business. One hour later, the real estate agent contacted me to say that two shops are now available, and I should come to view the one that I would like. When I returned, the gentleman that I met confessed that he was the Owner of the property. I could not believe it! The realtor told me that when I left, the owner told her to ensure that I was given one of the shops! I had to cry that day!!

Dear reader, do not doubt God! If He gives you an instruction—BE OBEDIENT! I resigned my job after getting the release from the Lord to do so. The peace that I felt while driving home that evening was because he had a bigger and better plan for me. I found favor through the Lord from the owner of that plaza that particular morning because I moved by faith. I am encouraging you to do the same thing—go to the Lord and find out what He wants you to do. After prayer, do not just sit there—you must move by faith! I decided to elaborate on this process because I know that there are quite a number of persons who are operating from a position of fear to take that bold step to just start.

Once the contract was signed, I started to work on the shop space with money that I had saved from my 9-5 job. I knew that I wanted to transition from my 9-5 job so I would always put some funds aside from my salary to fund my dream. Always put plans in place so that when the opportunity comes, you are ready! Do you have a 9-5 transition plan?

You Are One Decision Away

When you begin to see how powerful you are, self-investment will become a priority. You will no longer wonder if you can do it, but begin to say, "I Must Do It." Many people shy away from the decision to self-invest in the form of being an entrepreneur because they do not believe in themself. Are you ready to tap into the next version of yourself? Take some time to think now. What have you always wanted to venture into; that thing that makes your eyes light up when you speak about it? I challenge you today to start your self-investment journey by taking baby steps. Yes, start by doing some basic research on that brilliant idea. Start studying the area of interest and make some notes. In fact, go out and get a specific journal for those notes as soon as possible. The next thing to do is a business plan; get the ideas out of your head and put them on paper. You will then start feeling the energy to pursue with resilience. Look, just start small and take your time. If you are serious about starting your own business, believe me when I say that "it is possible". I registered my business, started to research the industry, did my business plan, started to save, started my social media pages and ventured out on

105

a small scale until I now own a store looking to open a second location. It is possible to own your own business, it is possible to transition from your 9-5. It is also possible to own your own business while you are in your 9-5. Say it with me – "it is possible".

Read! Read! Read!

I remember when I started my self-development journey some years ago. In fact, it is quite funny now that I am reflecting as I write this book. I had just gotten married, and my husband was in another country. Honestly, the journey started out of straight boredom (smile) or, should I say, God's divine plan for my life. I became a serial reader, and I can tell you that it changed my life. Are you going to feel like pulling yourself away from the crowd to carry out this valuable exercise? Absolutely not! But it is something you need to do to grow as an individual.

Reading stimulates your mind, reduces stress, and widens your knowledge and vocabulary. Everything you need to know about life is in a book somewhere. Why would you want to go through life's harsh experiences when you can read about what someone went through and learn from it so you don't make that same mistake?

Read to keep yourself informed of local and international events and read widely so you can contribute to a conversation from an intelligent place. Reading also keeps your brain working and therefore reduces the possibility of developing certain diseases.

You must prepare yourself for where you are going, and where you are going is bigger than where you are right now. You will travel locally and internationally, and you will meet new people of different cultures and backgrounds. Reading will help with your conversational skills. In order to pull your future into the present, you must read widely to dominate and take authority over your present situations. Okay, still sounds difficult? Why not start by inviting a friend to come on the journey with you. Pick a book and start by reading half of a page per night and have a short discussion with your friend the day after. The following night, try extending it to a page. Remember, this is your journey; you can decide to read once, twice, or three times per week. You can decide to read on a Wednesday only or every other night. That is doable, right? I wish you happy reading (smile).

CHAPTER 4
EMPOWERING SELF

Remain Self-Empowered

Self-empowerment means making a conscious decision to take charge of your destiny. It involves making positive choices, taking action to advance, and being confident in your ability to make and execute decisions. Self-empowered people understand their strengths and weaknesses and are motivated to learn and achieve. Self-empowerment allows individuals to recognize that they have the power to make choices that can help them achieve their goals. A self-empowered person is one who possesses inner strength and is intrinsically motivated. They do not rely on external forces to keep them going. The self-empowered persons hold themselves accountable for their own life. They control their atmosphere and who is in their space.

Step out of "feeling empowered" to "being empowered." To feel empowered can be alluded to listening to a motivational speech, and you feel ready to take action, but you do not have enough willpower to do so. To be empowered is when measurable actions are taken toward change or when there is a practical application. Personal empowerment is when you maintain strong self-confidence and self-esteem. It means giving yourself permission to simply be your brilliant self.

To have self-empowerment, you need to have a purpose, a reason, a cause, a "why" that underpins your actions. Getting clear about that is going to give you clarity in almost every area of your life because it gives you a filter with which to decide what you are willing to do or not to do.

Take Ownership of Your Inner-Power

Let us take some time and break out this sub-topic. Taking ownership means remaining accountable or taking responsibility of or for something. In this context, it means taking responsibility for who you are and who you are becoming. When one takes ownership of their power, they are using their God-given ability to exist, to overcome, to execute. Letting go of your inner power is a dangerous thing to do as the mind will lose clarity and confidence when weakened. Earlier in the book, we spoke about knowing who you are and the significance of basking in that knowing. One way to maintain your inner power is to know who you are and what you are about. For example, you may say to yourself, "I am a blessed child of God who receives favour everywhere I go" or "I am a successful entrepreneur who attracts people with a kingdom mindset." Always remind yourself of what the Word of God says about you and reiterate how great you are at what you do, whether you are a pastor, teacher, an accountant, a lawyer, an entrepreneur, etc. Affirmations placed in strategic locations, repeated daily, are sure ways to remind yourself.

Another way to take ownership of your inner power is to be comfortable with who you are. Knowing who you are is one thing, but are you comfortable with who you are? Whether you are an introvert or an extrovert, tall or short, black or white, it is important to be comfortable in your own skin. Do not compare yourself to anyone. Stay in your own lane and run your own race. When negative self-talk steps in, it breaks your confidence and robs you of your inner power.

Taking ownership of your inner power also means remaining bold and confident. In fact, confidence is the new attractive. When you walk into a room, do not dim your light to please anyone. Square your shoulder, walk tall, and just be your natural brilliant self. Why dim your light when the world needs you to shine? Stay in your inner power by knowing who you are, remaining comfortable with who you are and being bold and confident.

Lack Empowerment? Do Something About It!

Many times, we need to change "something" about "some things," but we sit and look at it as if it will change itself. Nothing changes unless you change it.

Your change is a decision away, and that decision lies with you. If you want to live the life you imagine that you can live, should live, or want to live, then you must be the one in control. If you don't feel empowered to direct and control your life, you will become dejected and drained to the point where you lose your drive and enthusiasm. You can find yourself in a barren land, living a "zombie" life. A zombie life is when one robotically and aimlessly lives their life without purpose.

"What if I cannot find the willpower to change my life?" The answer to that question lies in how much you love yourself. Do you love yourself enough to find the courage to fix the situation so you can move into your next season? It is not a matter of whether you want to do it or not – it is a must!

No matter what you are seeking—more wealth, less weight, a happier marriage, a better job—it can only happen if you do something about it. Tired of people treating you less than who you are? Do something about it. Tired of being in lack and feeling unhealthy? Do something about it. Want your kids to do their homework without being told? Do, well, that might be very difficult (smile), but you get the point. The point is, nothing changes if nothing changes. If you want something to be better, it is up to you to take the necessary steps to make it happen.

Self-Empowerment and Self-Confidence

There is a direct correlation between self-empowerment and self-confidence. An empowered person is the most confident person one will ever find. Self-empowered people take control of their lives by setting goals and taking actionable steps to achieve them. They not only understand how to get things done, but they are also confident, focused, and comfortable making decisions that guide them toward their future. The person who is not empowered often lacks confidence in themselves and their ability to make their own decisions.

The question is asked, can one be empowered all the time? Is that even possible? While we all know that all things are possible, I am not always empowered. I find that I am the least empowered when I lose my structure and routine, that is, my prayer, exercise, healthy eating, or book reading routines. My Morning Success Routine (MSR) is to wake up at 4 am, pray, read the Word, listen to something motivational, and exercise. My Night Success Routine (NSR) is to thoroughly cleanse my face of makeup, read, sit in meditation for fifteen minutes, and drink a cup of ginger tea. When I operate out of structure, I find myself enjoying very

114

unproductive days leading to disempowering feelings and thoughts. In the battlefield of your mind, you will begin to ask yourself questions and making statements such as:

1. Am I worthy of earning such a substantial amount of money.
2. Can I handle such a big account at my workplace?
3. I will never get that promotion.
4. I cannot write a book. I'm just not smart enough.
5. I don't have the ability to start and run my own business.
6. I have to stay in this abusive relationship. This is what I deserve; no other man or woman will want me.

When you are on the battlefield of your mind, you are in constant war with yourself, and it will ultimately drain you. Over time, you will become dis-empowered, and self-confidence goes with it as well.

Undoubtedly, it is very difficult to feel empowered when the struggles of life hit you upside the head. It is very difficult when you are not able to pay the rent or mortgage, the children cannot go to school, your car is giving problems, etc. It will make you want to stay locked in the house for days and pull the cover over your face in the mornings. That is quite understandable. I have a question for you though, what contribution have you made to your current state? What is happening right now, is it a direct result of the decisions that you made some time ago? Where can you take personal responsibility in the grand scheme of things? You see, it is very easy to remain dis-empowered; it is very easy to blame the world for what is happening around you, BUT what good is that doing for you? How does remaining in a dis-empowered state help you?

You must remain in control of your life. If you are not in control of your life, someone or something else will control your life for you. Yes, the government will, your children will, the difficult circumstances will, your husband or wife will. Who or what have you given the remote control to? Who or what has dis-empowered you? Think about it! Find the source and get your power back today! Once you find the source of your disempowered feeling and deal with it, you will find that your self-empowerment will return, and so will your self-confidence.

CHAPTER 5
EMPOWERED TO QUIT TOXICITY

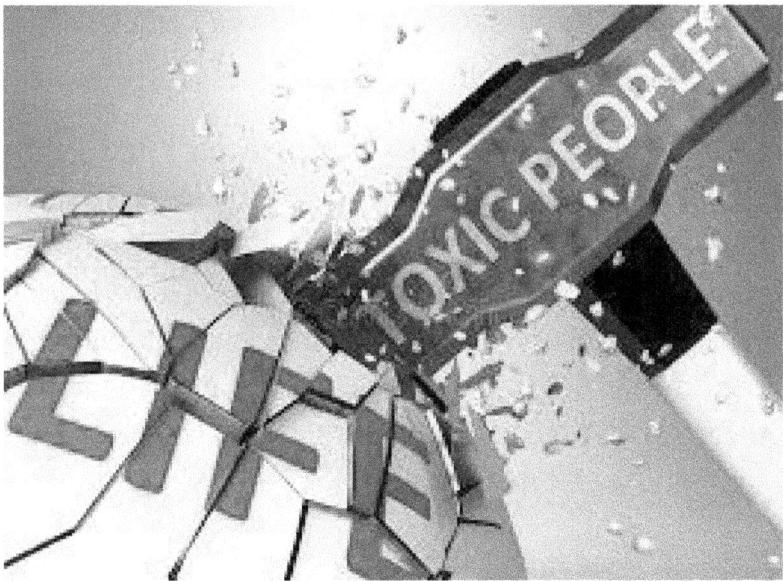

Knowing What You Want

If someone asked you this impromptu question, "What do you want out of life?", would you be able to properly articulate what those needs are immediately? The problem for a lot of people is that they do not know what they want. These are the individuals who are scattered in their thinking; indecisive and uncertain about what they want. Most people will say they want to be happy, but what does that look like? You must know what you want so when you get it, you know what it feels like.

You must know what your "negotiables" and "non-negotiables" are. Take some time out to understand what your blueprint is and why. A person's blueprint is what will bring joy and peace to their life. This will look different for everyone. For example, an individual's blueprint can be a loving marriage with a bunch of children, while another can be financial and personal freedom to travel the world.

There are some things that are tolerable for some, while it is non-negotiable for another. Do this activity for me; grab a book or a piece of paper and draw a line in the middle. At the top of the page, write NEGOTIABLE on one side and NON-NEGOTIABLE on the other. Begin to list as many things as possible, and study that list for a week. This list will become your blueprint. Finally, you are now in the know as to what is acceptable from what is not.

True empowerment comes from converting intention into action. You therefore cannot be truly empowered and remain empowered if you do not know what your own intentions are. The key is to identify what you want and intentionally move towards it. Track your small wins through persistence and resilience and see how empowered you feel at the end of each day as you check off your accomplishments from your to-do list.

While it is important to plan, things will not always go as planned. Situations and circumstances will arise that you do not like but imagine if you take the opportunity to ask yourself questions such as:

1. If this is not how I like it, how would I like it to be?
2. As this is not what I want, what do I want?
3. If this situation was the way I wanted it to be, how would it look, sound, and feel?
4. Given all the resources I needed to change this, what changes would I make?
5. How would I behave if I had this skill/trait? For example, confidence.

Ellecia Clarke-Edwards

Empowered to Quit Toxic Relationships

Most of us tend to resist change; it is a natural part of how we are made up. Something I have always maintained is that we must be present to what eventually becomes our norm. If your norm is to eat late at night when you get home, then your body will crave something to eat whether you are hungry or not. Similarly, if your norm is to have toxic people in your social and intimate space, then asking you to separate yourself from toxic people will be very difficult. It will be difficult because your mind has acclimatized itself to that norm and it has therefore become your reality. You will need a mindset shift to quit toxic relationships.

Being in a toxic relationship of any sort will bring disharmony to your space. What does it really mean to be in a toxic relationship? A toxin is poisonous—a substance that can cause illness, damage or even death. A toxic relationship, then, is one that is sick. It might even be dying. While we all have our moments and seasons of selfishness, a truly toxic person will pull from you and give you nothing in return. It is parasitic, where you feel like your energy is being drained. You find yourself serving someone at the expense of your feeling, need, and joy. Whether the relationship is a marriage, friend, work, etc., once there are signs of toxicity, it is very important to talk about it before resentment comes in.

Marriage Toxicity

Marriage relationships start out rich, healthy, and fun. So, ideally, the male proposes, the couple gets married, and they ride off into the sunset and live happily ever after. Oh yes, that is the way it should always be but, unfortunately, this does not happen all the time. In fact, the divorce rate is so high now that one can safely say it does not happen most of the time.

I personally believe that marriage is a beautiful thing; you get the opportunity to enjoy life with someone your heart adores. When you find someone who loves and supports you, I believe that is rare and must be cherished once it is found. Finding someone you have a strong chemistry and connection with is simply awesome. A man and a woman coming together to form a marriage relationship intimidate the devil because a marriage ordained by God is one that will accomplish the purpose of God. The Word of God says that "Two are better than one" (Ecclesiastes 4:9a - KJV). It also says that "One can chase a thousand but two can put ten thousand to flight" (see Deuteronomy 32:30). This is the reason why the enemy will attack marriages or any healthy social relationship. He knows there is power in numbers.

121

When a marriage starts to go downhill, the first spirit that we can speak to is a spirit of familiarity. Familiarity is having a deep understanding of someone or something that you lose that sense of admiration, respect, and awe. Familiarity leads to a lack of empathy and respect. It can be one partner demanding for the other to live up to their expectations, refusing to see things from their perspective, or just an inability to feel genuine understanding and compassion for the other person. When a relationship gets to this stage, it is a sure red flag that all is not well, and corrective actions must be taken as quickly as possible.

The spirit of familiarity is a sneaky and subtle spirit that can go easily unrecognized. Over time, the relationship moves from a high standard to medium to plain mediocre. Most couples do not realize this until it is too late, until there is a build-up of resentment and toxicity.

Why do individuals stay in toxic marriages? If something is not good for you, you would want to think that we all have the common sense to change to something that is better. We have seen it time and time again, where married couples remain in a toxic, nonchalant relationship for years, and the bystanders look on to say, "Why doesn't he or she just leave?" The truth is, while it seems simple for others to say, the parties involved may find it difficult because of a number of reasons, such as:

1. They have a bond with their partner (though it may be negative).
2. They have children together.
3. They share assets together that probably have to be sold and split.
4. The fear of being alone.
5. The fear of not finding love again.
6. The fear of being judged.
7. You have low self-esteem.
8. Financial constraints on the part of one partner.

The fact is, deep down, we want our relationships to work. Nobody wants to invest their time and effort with someone only to have it end after a few years. The mere thought of starting all over again is painful to think about, so many just go with the flow. When you spend time getting to know someone, you are naturally prone to fall into a certain comfort zone. Often times your comfort zone will keep you in places that are not good for you. When you feel comfortable, the thought of change brings anxiety and fear that you do not want to face head on. While I am not a marriage expert, and while all the reasons above are quite valid, it will all boil down to your level of self-love. Ultimately, it is up to the individual to weigh the pros and cons and make an informed decision. If you love yourself, you will choose "YOU" over the toxicity that you find yourself in.

Many people lose themselves in relationships without even realizing it, or when they do realize it, years have passed. With the passing years, resentment is built up, anger has taken over and they begin to operate out of character. Pay attention to the mind; it is a powerful tool. When one is in a toxic relationship, the individual will stay because they have conditioned their mind to that relationship. It is scary to think about leaving because it will shift them from their comfort zone into taking action. In a deliberate protest not to take action, they will sit in hope. They will hope they can change the person and things will get better over time. If you are in a toxic marriage, take some time to sit and talk with your partner.

So, you may say, "My partner is not physically abusing me, so I'm good. I wouldn't call that toxic." Well, toxicity can also mean emotional and mental abuse, even as seemingly small as the person not catering to your needs. Note that I said "seemingly small" because, in your mind, you may think that your needs are not important, but they are very important. If you are in a relationship where your partner consistently and deliberately takes you for granted and makes your desires seem trivial and insignificant, that will lead you to feel unworthy. Both partners should take some time to understand the needs and desires of the other partner. Both partners must have a common understanding of what the non-negotiables of the relationship are. For example, from day one, my husband and I spoke about cheating. We had that as a non-negotiable. We agreed that that was an unpardonable sin. My exact words were "I will not pardon that sin to continue in a marriage where cheating would have taken place. I will forgive, but I will release you from my life immediately." Open and honest communication is necessary in a marriage. God wants you to be in a loving and happy marriage, and you must be ready to have a conversation on that matter, even though it may be difficult to have.

After the conversation, then what? You can tell if someone is committed to growth. After each party comes clean about what their areas of concern are, the next step is to take action. Each party must do what they say they are going to do. They must also recognize and acknowledge their own personal issues and be ready to address them. Both parties must be committed to taking action toward a solution and be ready to work as a team. If you are in a mental, emotional, or physically toxic relationship, you must hold yourself accountable to your own self-care journey. You must position yourself to take the best care of yourself.

Don't Mold Your Partner in Your Image

I value this section of the book because the Lord made it possible for me to minister to many hurting, married women who have been hurt and disappointed in their marriages. The common thread in all the conversations with these women is that they felt they had given so much to their partner. They neglected themselves for their partner, and they have given up on their dream and purpose for their partner. I hastily reminded them that a marriage cannot be one-sided, and just as they are required to serve their husband, the husband is equally called to the serving table. It is important that both partners are serving each other and building each other up, helping each other to manifest purpose. The Word of God says, "Two are better than one...." (Ecclesiastes 4:9a) for a reason, and the scale should not be tipped toward the male or female in any order of significance.

When two people get married, it is two different personalities coming together to co-exist. We are all unique beings with different likes and dislikes, and each partner must develop a healthy appreciation of each other's uniqueness. The business of molding the other partner into your image is toxic and stressful. To evade that stress, communication is indeed mandatory. Lack of healthy communication can lead to a divorce. Can you imagine that simple things such as leaving the toilet seat up, not taking out the garbage, not squeezing the toothpaste from the bottom are causing quarrels and resentment? When this continues over a period of time, it leads to divorce.

Being married now for over five years, I have learned that you don't have to create a "big deal" over minuscule things. If my husband does not take the garbage out, I merely remind him to do so. Believe me though, it was not always like that (smile). In my relationship, I am always the structured type who has systems in place to remain on top of my game and be productive. My husband is the complete opposite and is very laid back. It took clear and concise communication about our personalities for us to now have a healthy appreciation for the unique beings that we are.

Always seek to maintain your God-given individuality. What do I mean by this? We all have aspects of our character that we need to work on. As you enter that marital home, ask yourself "What can I work on to become the best version of myself in this relationship?" While it is important to maintain your individuality in your relationship, there may be aspects of your "individuality" that may be toxic to your marriage. Have you ever heard of a person who said they have been an angry or aggressive person all their life and they can't change? They have concluded in their mind that "a so mi tan." If you take this side of you into marriage and continue with that narrative, it will affect the prosperity of your marriage. Therefore, it is your God-given individuality that must be maintained—that part of you that is manifesting the fruit of the Spirit: "…love, joy, peace, longsuffering, gentleness, goodness, faith, meekness, temperance…"(see Galatians 5:22-23).

Marriage is such a beautiful thing that ought to be honoured and cherished. However, that beautiful thing can become very toxic if attention is not placed on caring for each other's well-being.

Empowered to Quit Toxic WorkPlaces

Toxicity is when something becomes harmful to your overall well-being. Dear reader, I need you to take some time and examine if your job is toxic. Do you feel so overwhelmed at work that you feel like you want to pull your hair out? This question is also being posed to the entrepreneur. Let me tell you this, no job or business is worth you developing a chronic condition or that lands you in a hospital bed. The aim of one wanting to excel at something is to be able to enjoy it! If you work yourself sick to move up the corporate ladder or to get that business off the ground, how will you enjoy it? Sounds like the scripture "gaining the whole world and losing your soul" (see Mark 8:36). Why would you want to gain the whole world but lose your health?

Let us now balance the conversation. Working assiduously is mandatory for the accomplishment of your goals, dreams, and desires. Any successful person being interviewed will tell you of the hard work and dedication they had to invest to see their current return. I can tell you about hard work. When I started my banking career in 2006, I made up my mind that I wanted to become a Branch Manager, and it was ready, set, go for me! The possibilities were endless, and I worked very hard to get to the level of a Business Banking Officer. The natural progression was from Telling to Customer Service Representative to Personal Banking Officer to Business Banking Officer and then to Branch Manager. I worked so hard that I skipped the Personal Banking Officer level and progressed from CSR to Business Banking. I know what it is like to be in corporate and being hungry for success! However, working hard to achieve your goals must be balanced with wanting to live to enjoy the fruits of your labour. Ecclesiastes 3:13 says "...every man should eat and drink, and enjoy the good of his labour..." (KJV). This can be translated to: When you work hard, "cock up yu foot!" (Lol). So, certainly, work hard, be the boss, be your excellent brilliant self. However, manage yourself well, and balance your game as you move toward the

129

accomplishment of your goals and the acquisition of wealth. Therefore, if you are a reader who has a 9-5 job that is becoming toxic, take some time and read this section again. After you are through, start making some solid commitments to yourself. You know exactly what you need to do. You merely need to decide to work smarter and not harder (time management), or it may just be the time to quit that toxicity.

Self-Care and the Corporate Community

As I wrote this section of the book, a flood of memories was hitting me of when I worked at the bank. At that time, if you asked me what self-care is, I would be like, "What? What do you mean self-care? What is that?" My corporate hat was on so tight that all I thought about was work. My life was pretty much work, work, work. I would be the first person at work (arriving at 7 am), and my lunchtime would be 3 pm or 4 pm. Think about this, if you walk through the door at 5 pm while working in banking, your colleagues will look at you strangely. Yes, my departure time would be up to 8:30 pm at times. Some nights, while heading home, I would simply grab something on the road to eat. As a single professional who had her eyes on the prize to climb the corporate ladder through diligent work, I was convinced I was killing it. I was certainly in an empowered state. I remember using the term "intrinsically motivated" to describe myself a lot. I needed no external force to remain motivated.

After years of "killing work," I realized that the work was out to kill me! As I reflect now, I thank God I did not develop any serious health condition except a stomach burn. This happened as a result of not eating on time because I was so focused on slaying those goals.

I share this story because this is the reality of many. If you are a young professional who is genuinely ambitious and wants to excel in your career, I understand what that is like, but be sure not to do it at the expense of your health. If you are not in that season of your life and know of someone that this section of the book speaks to, get them a copy, or share this information with them as a reminder. We must NEVER compromise our health in the name of ambition. Seek to achieve some semblance of balance in your life.

For many, the quest becomes a race against time, "I must get this promotion before I get to a certain age." I fully understand this too. The person who remains in relentless pursuit without taking their health into consideration will, unfortunately, end up in a hospital bed. They will be reflecting on all that hard work without proper self-care that landed them right where they are. Do you know what comes upon you at that time? One word, "REGRET!" Oh, sorry, I didn't say that right, "A lot of GUILT and REGRET." Unfortunately, as well, this is the time when you play the "shoulda/woulda" game. I should have rested more; I should have spent more time with my family; I should have resigned when I saw that the job got too toxic; I should have left work earlier; I should have gone to lunch earlier. The worst thing that one can do is to live their life in regret.

Self-care is undoubtedly lacking in the corporate community. It is possible to balance your time so you can enjoy your personal life and your work life. When it is all said and done, you are unable to enjoy any aspect of your life unless your health is intact. Remain empowered and in control of your life by practicing proper self-care while basking in your corporate affairs.

The Self-Care and Work-Life Balancing Game

When I resigned from my job in 2017, my world did not fall apart. In fact, I travelled and started a totally new journey. When I returned to Jamaica, I picked up my career in Sales Management. I spoke about this in detail in my first book "Two Kingdom Keys To Success: Mind Elevation and Spiritual Alertness." It was actually when I resigned and looked back at my banking journey that I realized the risk I took with my health. I thank

God for His grace in keeping me at that time. I certainly started to operate from a place of wisdom when I resumed my career in Sales Management and started to go back to school. The Lord had done some serious work on me when I travelled, so I was operating from a place of heightened consciousness. I certainly wanted to accomplish my goals, but I also wanted to live out my purpose. As I said in an earlier chapter, when you have a clear understanding of PURPOSE, you become even more excited to LIVE. When you link self-care to your purpose, you will begin to take your self-care journey more seriously.

There are only 24 hours in one day, so how do I get all this work done and still find time to practice self-care? I know this question would come. There are 24 hours in a day, and proper planning of your day can lead to super productive days and, yes, time will be there for self-care. Time is always there! Why do I say this? *Because we will always make time for the things that are important to us.*

Here are some helpful tips on how a Corporate Professional/Entrepreneur can have maximum productivity:

- Plan for your day the day before.

- If you are in Sales, plan your road days and book as many face-to-face appointments for those days. Be sure to prospect per area.
- Implement power hours in your days. For example, between 10 am–12 noon for cold calls. Lock yourself into those two hours without any form of distraction. Take lunch immediately after, then return and respond to emails. Figure out the routine that works best for you and stick to that success routine.
- Isolate yourself from distractions. For example, your cell phone can be your biggest distraction.
- Get restful sleep at night. You must rest your brain to breathe creativity the following day.
- Feed your mind with motivational, inspirational, and transformational food every day. Make it a part of your morning success routine.
- Properly hydrate yourself, and do not eat junk food. Junk food is one of the biggest stealers of your energy.
- Exercise daily for a minimum of 15-20 minutes. If not daily, exercise three times per week. Remember, this can be just going for a walk; it does not have to be rigorous exercise. Study your body and know what works for you.
- Entrepreneurs, rally the team around you and learn the art of delegation.

- Professionals, engage your team members and let them know how they can assist you in achieving your sales target. Conversely, let them know how you can assist them. Team effort is needed as you cannot achieve greatness on your own.

- Wake up early. Does 4 pm or 5 pm work for you? Waking up early means you are already ahead of the game. It gives you more time to work out, plan your day, work on business, and be more productive. Create a morning success routine that works for you.

- Write down your thoughts before bed. Writing before bed will improve your quality of sleep. When you journal your thoughts, it allows you to put things into perspective. Take the thoughts out of your head and get them organized on paper. You will then engage in better and proper planning, which will result in a more structured day.

Will there be days when you must work beyond five? Definitely, but you must make a conscious effort not to make it a habit. For example, you can work beyond 5 pm on Mondays and Wednesdays. You can use your early days to go to the gym, get a massage, spend time with the kids, plan a romantic night out with your partner, go to the movies, or whatever else you like to do. These activities, for some, are very relaxing and therefore fall in the self-care category. Remember, *self-care is the practice of taking an active role in protecting your own well-being, pursuing happiness, and having the ability, tools, and resources to respond to periods of stress so that they don't result in imbalance and lead to a health crisis.* Self-care is not about being selfish. It allows you to make your greatest contribution to the world. Proper self-care re-charges, refreshes, rejuvenates, and re-energizes us from the core of our hearts.

PART B

CHAPTER 6
SELF-CARE AND THE WORD

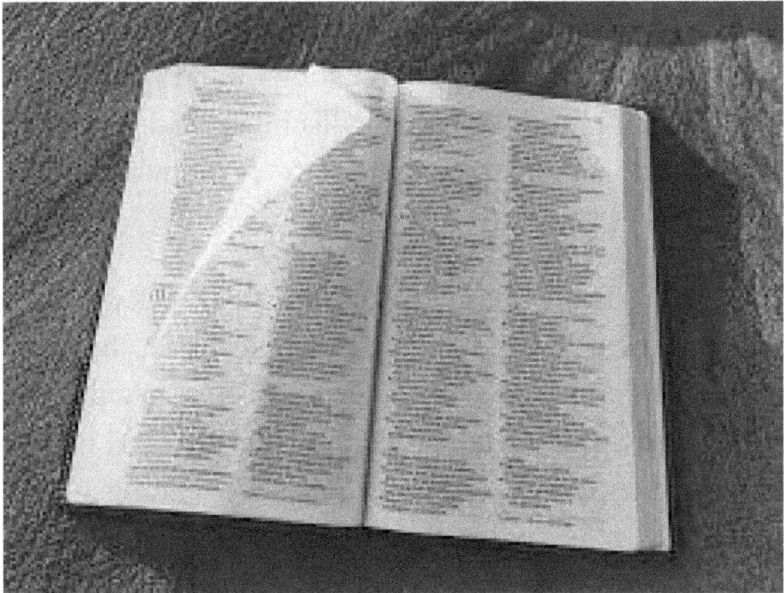

Does the Bible speak about self-care? The Bible does not explicitly speak about self-care; however, there are scriptures that speak to taking care of one's mental, emotional, spiritual, and physical well-being. While we cannot pinpoint where self-care is mentioned anywhere in the Bible, we know that Jesus took Himself away from the crowds to be alone with the Father to pray (see Luke 5:16). We cannot speak to anything else that was done during that time, but we can conclude that when He returned, He was full to continue doing what He was called to do. Genesis 2:2-3 speaks to God resting on the 7th day. We also see that He cared that His disciples "had no leisure even to eat" and instructed them to "rest a while." (see Mark 6:31).

Though the Bible does not categorically break out self-care in terms of the different aspects of life, there are scriptures that speak to the varied aspects. Note that the Bible does speak to taking care of our physical bodies as it is a temple, guarding our hearts, tending to our spirits, and renewing our minds.

Physical Self-Care

Taking care of our physical body, though it is the vehicle to our purpose, is normally the last thing on our "To-do list." Ironic, right? Physical self-care speaks to good nutrition, sufficient amount of recovery time (rest and sleep), and exercise. It speaks to making sure that your body is well-nourished and happy. Even though we have very busy schedules, it is important that we get all three things in. Having a healthy body is key to living a fulfilling life. Take care of your body or someone will take care of it for you. Here are some scriptures that speak to physical self-care:

1 Corinthians 10:31 (NLT): "So whether you eat or drink, or whatever you do, do it all for the glory of God."

1 Corinthians 3:17 (NLT): "God will destroy anyone who destroys this temple. For God's temple is holy, and you are that temple."

Ephesians 5:18 (NLT): "Don't be drunk with wine, because that will ruin your life. Instead, be filled with the Holy Spirit."

Romans 12:1 (NLT): "And so, dear brothers and sisters, I plead with you to give your bodies to God because of all he has done for you. Let them be a living and holy sacrifice—the kind he will find acceptable. This is truly the way to worship him."

Ephesians 5:29 (NLT): "No one hates his own body but feeds and cares for it, just as Christ cares for the church."

Mental Self-Care

Mental health includes emotional, psychological, and social well-being. It affects how we think, feel, act, make choices, and relate to others. Mental health is more than the absence of a mental illness—it is essential to your overall health and quality of life. Self-care can play a role in maintaining your mental health. This dimension of self-care is all about looking after your mental well-being (your thoughts and feelings).

Mental self-care also involves training your mind. We must feed our physical bodies to keep it fit; it is the same way we need to train and feed our minds with strong motivational, inspirational, and transformational food. A sharp mind makes you more capable of dealing with stress and equips you to navigate life's changes. Your paradigm and your perception of the world is affected by your thoughts and feelings. Therefore, you must be mindful of your inner dialogue.

Any activity that declutters your mind and reduces stress is mental self-care. Exercise, learning something new, and meditation are sure means of healthy mental care. With there being so many distractions around us, it is imperative to build mental fitness and avoid people, circumstances, and situations that create mental exhaustion.

Some great mental care practices include:

- Focusing your attention on the present moment.
- Practicing gratitude.
- Exercising patience over hurrying to "have things done."
- Practicing acceptance of what is already happening.

Talk to Someone

Mental health is a topic that has a stigma associated with it. When one speaks about mental health, it is automatically assumed that the person has some form of psychological issue. Therefore, many are afraid to express themselves when they are not feeling well mentally. It is important that you start monitoring your own self-care and remove the stigma for your own benefit.

Here are some scriptures that speak to mental self-care:

Philippians 4:8 (NLT): "...Fix your thoughts on what is true, and honorable, and right, and pure, and lovely, and admirable. Think about things that are excellent and worthy of praise."

Romans 8:6 (NLT): "So letting your sinful nature control your mind leads to death. But letting the Spirit control your mind leads to life and peace."

Isaiah 26:3 (NLT): "You will keep in perfect peace all who trust in you, all whose thoughts are fixed on you."

Emotional Self-Care

Emotional well-being focuses on bringing awareness to your emotional needs by becoming conscious of your feelings. This awareness allows you to process your feelings in a healthy way, focusing on the positive emotions and managing the negative ones. These are some powerful ways to improve your emotional health:

- Meditate
- Practice gratitude
- Practice self-compassion
- Observe your thoughts without judging
- Use deep breathes to regulate emotions
- Do acts of kindness
- Start journaling

Emotional self-care helps you respond rather than react to life's challenges. Responding means you are

144

measured and thoughtful when you approach a situation. Reacting, on the other hand, is an immediate emotional response that usually results in a negative outcome. God cares about our emotions and how we react to them. Do not let your emotions fool you; the Bible charges us to keep our emotions under control.

Here are some Bible scriptures on emotional self-care:

Proverbs 17:22 (NLT): "A cheerful heart is good medicine, but a broken spirit saps a person's strength."

Proverbs 16:32 (NLT): "Better to be patient than powerful; better to have self-control than to conquer a city."

Romans 15:13 (NLT): "I pray that God, the source of hope, will fill you completely with joy and peace because you trust in him. Then you will overflow with confident hope through the power of the Holy Spirit."

Spiritual Self-Care

Spiritual self-care is any activity that we undertake to grow our faith and who we truly are. This part of ourselves is the REAL us, driven by our deep desires and what matters most to us at our core. Practicing spiritual self-care not only leads to greater inner peace, but it can help us live in greater alignment with our core values. Spiritual self-care is soul-fulfilling, encourages introspection, and offers clarity and comfort.

Finding time for spiritual self-care has a number of health benefits. It quiets the mind and helps to calm the turbulence within, leaving space to begin feeling and honouring what the heart yearns for, and having the courage to take the necessary actions for change.

There are many ways to stay connected. Two such ways to stay connected are to:

1. Keep plugged into the divine source through prayer.
2. Practicing forgiveness.

Staying Plugged In

After praying one beautiful morning, I laid down on the couch to be in quietness to hear what God was saying. I laid in a position where the clock was staring right at me. I looked intently and noticed how the clock was ticking away. The clock was on the wall fulfilling its purpose of giving time. The only thing that could stop the ticking clock was if you removed the power source, the battery. Similarly, when you use your phone all day, you need to plug the phone in and leave it plugged into the source. I started to liken this to us as human beings; if you do not stay plugged into the one and only source

(God), you will stop manifesting purpose. Just as the phone continues to lose battery life if it is not plugged into the source (the socket), it is the same way we need to sit down in quietness and get recharged by plugging into the heavenly with prayer and constant dialogue with God. We must stay plugged into our source so we can become recharged and re-energized daily. This is a powerful form of self-care.

Practice Forgiveness

Forgiveness is a needed medicine for life and for the sustenance of our souls. The Word of God says that we need to forgive seventy times seven times (see Matthew 18:22). This means that we must be open to forgiving others, even when we consider it to be difficult. Note that there are people who will intentionally do you wrong and quote this scripture in an effort to weasel their way back into your life. I am not talking about people who are deliberately malicious to you. There comes a time in a man or a woman's life when you must make the firm decision to cut some persons from your life who are becoming toxic.

Do not allow others to steal your inner peace and joy. It is your vehicle of strength. If someone did something to you that you deem unforgiveable, go deep within your soul, and acknowledge how you feel. Cry about it if you must, but learn to forgive quickly so it does not create disharmony, resentment, bitterness, anger, etc. This is toxic to your system and will create harm for you while the aggressor is sleeping quite well at night. Unforgiveness is not worth it; it will hinder your spiritual growth! Forgive and move on. Jot down forgiveness under your spiritual self-care plan.

Spiritual self-care can help you to:

- Improve relationships and connection with others.
- Experience more inner peace.
- Deepen relationship with self and enhances feelings of oneness.
- Gain clarity on what makes you happy.

Here are some scriptures on spiritual self-care:

1 Thessalonians 5:23 (NLT): "Now may the God of peace make you holy in every way, and may your whole spirit and soul and body be kept blameless until our Lord Jesus Christ comes again."

2 Peter 3:18a (NLT): "Rather, you must grow in the grace and knowledge of our Lord and Savior Jesus Christ."

2 Timothy 3:16-17 (NLT): "All Scripture is inspired by God and is useful to teach us what is true and to make us realize what is wrong in our lives. It corrects us when we are wrong and teaches us to do what is right. God uses it to prepare and equip his people to do every good work."

2 Peter 1:5-8 (NLT): "In view of all this, make every effort to respond to God's promises. Supplement your faith with a generous provision of moral excellence, and moral excellence with knowledge, and knowledge with self-control, and self-control with patient endurance, and patient endurance with godliness, and godliness with brotherly affection, and brotherly affection with love for everyone. The more you grow like this, the more productive and useful you will be in your knowledge of our Lord Jesus Christ."

Financial Self-Care

Your financial well-being is an essential aspect of your life and profoundly affects your security and overall happiness. Practicing financial self-care means focusing your time and energy on your money situation, making concrete plans and goals to cultivate a better financial future, and finding ways to support a healthy money mindset.

Practicing self-care in the various aspects of life is critical and financial self-care is an aspect that is often overlooked. If your expenses are more than your income, there is a real cause for concern. Soon, you will start feeling overwhelmed. You must position yourself financially and recognize when you need to shift your mindset. When the COVID-19 pandemic hit, the vaccine became mandatory at my 9-5 job, and I decided to resign my job. This was one month after my long-awaited dream manifested of opening a retail hair, beauty, and cosmetic store. Given that I was now in full-time entrepreneurship, I knew I needed to revisit my money mindset and look at money from a different perspective, meaning, from an entrepreneurial perspective.

Money From an Entrepreneurial Mindset

Moving into full-time entrepreneurship demanded another version of myself. Though I was always very disciplined and structured with money, I needed to approach money management from a different perspective. How did I do this? I started to implement systems to separate my business from personal money. This was especially essential for tax purposes and to prepare me for future banking transactions for business expansion.

Shifting my mindset to an entrepreneurial perspective also resulted in me seeing money from a "light place." This means that I stopped hunting it and started to attract it. Oh yes, this was a revelation for me, and when I started to see clients calling me for my store products and to be a part of my coaching programs, I knew something had happened. I had released my hold of it and allowed the wealth that comes from God to find me. When you speak God's promises over your life and business and start working on becoming a person of value, everything will shift.

How did I take action on my newfound mindset, you may ask? I started to take myself out on CEO lunches and weekends to unwind. You see, when you do this, you are building up yourself to attract more. Getting back to some of the foundational things that bring you joy and laughter is a significant aspect of financial self-care.

Irrespective of the season you are in right now, the time to start managing your financial health is now. Are you feeling overwhelmed financially? It is a sign that you need to sit down and evaluate your financial health. Whether you have a 9-5 or you are an entrepreneur, look at where you are on the financial self-care scale. Don't underestimate the impact that true financial peace can have on your overall mental health.

Understand that "treating yourself" is more than taking a trip to the spa or indulging in an exquisite meal. Sure, those things are important, but in terms of your finances, self-care means reevaluating your relationship with money, saving, and investing to pave the way for a brighter, more secure future.

Financial Distress: The Physical and Mental Effect

Money is tied to our basic hard-wired drive to survive, and when that drive can't be attained, it can compound into stress. Maybe it is why the age-old saying "Health is wealth" is more than just a cliché. Year after year, there is a rise in physical health issues, and this can be associated with financial distress and an impoverished society.

Signs of financial stress can include:

- Worrying and feeling anxious about money.
- Arguing with loved ones about money.
- Feeling guilty when you spend money on non-essential items.
- Being afraid to answer the phone or open your email.

Financial stress manifests itself in numerous physical conditions, like mood disorders, migraines, cardiovascular disease, insomnia, and more. Being in a perpetual state of unease and anxiety about finances, like when a person is living paycheck to paycheck, increases the body's cortisol levels and puts them at risk for:

- Anxiety and depression
- Digestive problems
- Headaches
- Heart disease
- Sleep problems
- Weight gain
- Memory and concentration impairment

There is a strong correlation between financial stress and mental health. If you are finding it difficult to meet your current expenses or are worried about your current or future finances, you are under <u>financial stress</u>. Like other types of stress, financial stress has two components:

- **objective** financial difficulty, where you don't have enough funds to cover necessary expenses or debts.
- **subjective** perceptions about your current or future finances, leading to worry and distress.

These two are related, but someone can have trouble meeting their expenses, view this as acceptable, and not be overly worried. Alternatively, someone may be reasonably financially secure but still feel quite stressed about their finances. Both instances do result in stress and distress that can be deleterious to your health. The key is to find a place of peace with money through proper planning, structure, and discipline. I recommend that you use the financial self-care checklist below to beat anxiety and find yourself in a more balanced and peaceful place.

Financial Self-care Checklist

1. **Create a budget.** Yes, you need one. Think of it as a way of controlling where your money goes, not restricting it. If your money has a plan, you will be able to do more with it and it works for you.

2. **Track your spending.** This is tied to having a budget because once you can see where you are spending money unnecessarily, you can adjust your spending habits to reign in the areas that need it.

3. **Open an Entertainment Account.** Once you are feeling stable and comfortable with your spending habits, allocate money in your budget for the occasional treat and reward your positive

financial moves. Take yourself out with friends and family to unwind and clear your mind.

4. **Set goals for your future spending habits.** Dream big because these dreams are what will motivate you to work towards your goals and maintain a healthy financial self-care routine. Every day, write down your goals, visualize them, and say them over in your head—what you water will grow.

5. **Start an Emergency Fund.** From the little to the big, unexpected expenses or income loss can have a big impact on your finances. Car expenses, vet bills, job loss, and more are the unfortunate reality of life, and it is likely that you will go through something at some point that is costly and unexpected. Aim for three to six months of your take-home pay, and while that may seem like a lot, it is okay to start small.

6. **Start Saving/Investing toward your goals.** Sometimes this means digging in the couch for spare change to put away, and that is a good place to start. Every bit of savings counts. The practice of putting money away on a regular basis is

important. The more you do it, the easier it will be to do it.

7. **Know where you lack financial literacy.** We all lack knowledge somewhere in the realm of financial literacy; there is so much to know! The good news is, there are countless resources available to help you brush up on your knowledge. Figure out what you need to know, and then take the time to figure it out or source out what you need.

8. **Pay off debt as quickly as possible.** Prioritize your debt payments and put deliberate steps in place to pay them off.

Take some time to review this checklist daily and stay on the path to a brighter financial future.

Here are some scriptures on financial self-care:

Ecclesiastes 5:19 (NLT): "And it is a good thing to receive wealth from God and the good health to enjoy it. To enjoy your work and accept your lot in life—this is indeed a gift from God."

1 Timothy 6:9-10a (NLT): "But people who long to be rich fall into temptation and are trapped by many foolish and harmful desires that plunge them into ruin and

156

destruction. For the love of money is the root of all kinds of evil."

Proverbs 23:4 (NLT): *"*Don't wear yourself out trying to get rich. Be wise enough to know when to quit."

Proverbs 3:9 (NLT): *"*Honor the Lord with your wealth and with the best part of everything you produce."

Self-Care Plan

To sum up this section of the book, I encourage you to make a SELF-CARE PLAN. This is a plan that breaks down what the key things are that must be done under each aspect of one's life. Adherence to a self-care plan takes dedication and consistency to work.

Keep your plan simple, and choose the self-care activities you love. Doing things that bring you joy is the key to sticking to your routine. Your self-care plan can also be as flexible as you need it to be. You will have your good days and your bad days. Don't be too hard on yourself when things don't go as planned. You can always have a fresh start.

Give yourself the kindness you deserve and build your own self-care plan today, OR you can just adopt mine…(smile).

Self-Care Plan

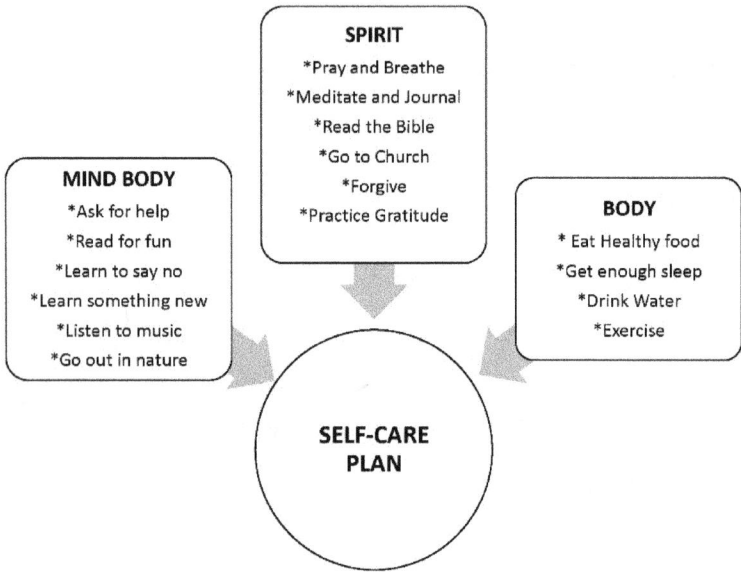

SPIRIT
*Pray and Breathe
*Meditate and Journal
*Read the Bible
*Go to Church
*Forgive
*Practice Gratitude

MIND BODY
*Ask for help
*Read for fun
*Learn to say no
*Learn something new
*Listen to music
*Go out in nature

BODY
* Eat Healthy food
*Get enough sleep
*Drink Water
*Exercise

SELF-CARE PLAN

Ask Yourself:

1. What activities bring me joy?
2. What helps me feel energized?
3. When do I feel at peace?
4. What makes me feel fulfilled?
5. What has helped me cope with difficult moments in my life?

158

Implement Systems That Work

For your plans to work, you must be deliberate and intentional. You must also put systems in place to ensure that they work. Having success routines will allow you to build momentum over time. Your self-care plan can be broken down to look something like what I will outline below. While it may not be as detailed as this one, you should seek to have a mental image of what your morning, afternoon, evening, and night success routines are.

Morning Before Work

- Awake and take a deep breath (breathe in and out slowly) (Physical).
- Do a morning prayer/reflection (Spiritual).
- Set your intentions for the day for how you want to be (emotional/cognitive) (Spiritual).
- Do thirty minutes of stretches/yoga (physical, emotional/cognitive).
- Drink a large glass of water (physical).
- Eat a healthy breakfast (physical).

Morning at Work

- Greet at least three people with a smile and "good morning." (social, emotional).
- Ask someone how they are doing before talking with them about work. (Social).
- Use the stairs not the elevator throughout the day. (Physical).
- Check your fluid consumption. (Physical).

Noon at Work

- Eat lunch. (Physical).
- Check your fluid consumption. (Physical).
- Do a breathing exercise. (Physical, Emotional).

Afternoon at Work

- Greet at least three people with a smile and a "good afternoon." (Social, Emotional).
- Check your fluid consumption. (Physical).

Evening Preparing to Leave Work

- Do a "Three Good Things" review of the workday. (Emotional/Cognitive).
- Set your intention for how you want to be during the evening. (Emotional/Cognitive).

- Do a breathing set (three times) before leaving work. (Physical, Emotional).
- Check your fluid consumption/go to the gym. (Physical).

Evening at Home

- Greet the people in your home and spend at least five minutes with them before doing anything else. Do this greeting via phone, video call, or social media if your family/friends live elsewhere. (Social, Emotional).
- Change out of your "work uniform" into home clothes (not pajamas) to help make the mental shift from workday to home time. (Emotional/Cognitive).
- Eat dinner mindfully at least 2-3 hours before going to bed. (Physical).
- Complete all screen time activities at least 15-30 minutes before going to bed. (Physical).
- Check to see if you have met your walking goal. (Physical).
- Go to bed at approximately the same time each night. (Physical).
- At bedtime, do a reflection/prayer. Reflect on your day's intentions for how you wanted to be that day. Do a "Three Good Things" review of

the day, including how you did with your self-care plan. Write down what you are grateful for. (Emotional/Cognitive, Spiritual).

Conclusion

Congratulations!

You have successfully completed the book, and I do hope you found great value in it. Now I have a question for you: When are you going to take your self-care journey seriously? I know it is easier to grab something on the road while driving home—it is easier than cooking—and I know that after a long workday, maybe you will want to forgo the gym and head home to get some rest. However, if you should go to the doctor after not feeling well, guess what, the doctor will tell you to do the same thing you already know you should be doing.

It is now time for you to get uncomfortable and start living a PROACTIVE LIFESTYLE instead of a REACTIVE one. Start meal prepping and start employing proper time management skills so you have time to go do your workout, start going to bed on time, etc. Look, failure to do these things will only lead to regret in the future. Your answer to the question that I posed just now should be a resounding "TODAY! Yes, I will start taking my self-care journey seriously today!"

Repeat after me:

- Taking care of myself is my responsibility because it is necessary for the manifestation of my purpose.
- I am the first and most important person in my life.
- I will make my dream come true.
- I accept my body and my complexion.
- I am powerful enough to change my today.
- I deserve the best and finest things in life.
- I will take care of myself every second of my life.
- I will not allow negative emotions to drive my mind.
- I will choose to love and respect myself.
- I will remember the importance of silence.
- I am ready to be healed and grow; I am doing my best.

I do encourage you to gift someone a copy of this book, and since you may have journaled some information in this one, keep it for future reference.

There were some valuable points mentioned throughout the book, and I have created a quick reference sheet just for you. Repetition solidifies your thoughts in the mind, so keep the book close so you can remind yourself of some key self-care tips daily.

Reminder Tips on Self-care

1. Prioritize sleep. Your mood and immune system are counting on it.
1. Know your personal signs of stress.
2. Skip, jump, hop, and get silly.
3. Avoid mindless snacking; eat intuitively instead.
4. Reach for high-protein snacks when you need an energy boost.
5. Meal prep. for ease of preparation when ready.
6. Add more fruits and veggies to your day.
7. Cook yourself a nourishing meal; minimize dining out.
8. Give yourself a meditation break.
9. Try chillaxing with your favourite music.
10. Relax with a book/audiobook.
11. Practice mindful listening.
12. Schedule a "Me" day.
13. Call a friend or family member just to talk.
14. Avoid nonstop news consumption.
15. Do positive affirmations daily.
16. Declutter your space.
17. Enroll in a course that you have always wanted to learn.
18. Be your authentic self; speak your mind.

19. Go get your hair, manicure, and pedicure done.
20. Do the work. Don't be lazy.
21. Stop waiting. Plan, Pray, and Take Action.
22. Rely on yourself. Your success depends on you.
23. Be practical in your doing. Success is not a theory.
24. Be productive early. Don't be lounging around all day wanting to feel productive.
25. Stop playing the victim and the blame game. Life is hard; level up!
26. Don't hang out with unproductive people.
27. Don't waste your energy on stuff you can't control.
28. Stop crying about the past; you can't do anything about it anyways.
29. Stop seeking approval from everyone. It makes no sense; you can't please everyone.
30. Stop putting junk food in your body. It is poison and you will die from it.
31. Stop doing the same things and hope that things will change.
32. Improve your mental diet.
33. Learn to let people down.
34. Set boundaries and protect them.
35. Replace or dismiss what is not working.
36. Look forward to your future, not back at your past.

37. Upgrade your library.
38. Stop self-rejecting.

APPENDIX

- https://erlc.com/resource-library/articles/what-does-the-bible-say-about-the-self-care-movement/

- https://www.bupa.co.uk/newsroom/ourviews/nine-benefits-good-night-sleep

- https://www.helpguide.org/articles/diets/emotional-eating.htm

- https://www.foodbev.com/news/confused-consumers-how-the-food-industry-can-help-support-informed-purchasing-decisions/

- https://www.scientificworldinfo.com/2020/10/importance-of-time-in-human-life.html

- https://www.ramseysolutions.com/relationships/toxic-relationship-signs

- https://www.marshfieldclinic.org/education/residents-and-fellows/well-being-committee/well-being-topics/quality-of-life/self-care-plans-building-yours

- https://www.bromwichandsmith.com/financial-self-care-checklist

www.ingramcontent.com/pod-product-compliance
Lightning Source LLC
Chambersburg PA
CBHW051835090426
42736CB00011B/1820